The Fifth Veda

Orange Books Publication

1st Floor, Rajhans Arcade, Mall Road, Kohka, Bhilai, Chhattisgarh 490020

Website: **www.orangebooks.in**

© Copyright, 2024, Author

All rights reserved. No part of this book may be reproduced, stored in a retrieval system, or transmitted, in any form by any means, electronic, mechanical, magnetic, optical, chemical, manual, photocopying, recording or otherwise, without the prior written consent of its writer.

First Edition, 2024

ISBN: 978-93-6554-455-8

THE FIFTH VEDA

ANOOP PRABHU

OrangeBooks Publication
www.orangebooks.in

Acknowledgements

I am deeply indebted to my parents for giving me a good schooling and childhood, my better half for her seemless support in editing and my sister for her words of energy and enthusiasm.

Special thanks to all my teacher's of literature and spirituality.

I also thank my blue light in guiding me.

Prologue

Today- T Nagar- Chennai.

Alarm bell rang at 5 AM. Mind never work when there is an early morning flight waiting. Message from boss regarding an important assignment deleted my sleep last night. Chief Editor, Mr. Ram has a compliant. Having brotherly affection, his mandate is to work on critical projects and earn laurels. According to him, I am an underdog in my profession. This is not because of the incapacity but due to inherent laziness. I have listened to this nonsense several times from school days. Teachers at SB college asked me to work for a university rank but I just secured a distinction. For me, passion and profession are overlapping. This is a wonderful recipe for a balanced life. Major share of my time is allocated to family and reading.... You may judge the reasons for Ram's anger.

The flight at 7 AM to Mumbai is always crowded. The taxi driver has the craft of making me reach the airport on time. Being a regular visitor to airport makes me a familiar face among security staff.

I have very less information regarding my current work. Ram has promised to appraise me with details once I reach Delhi. He studied in my senior batch for journalism. He has the habit of doing pranks. Last year he called me to Mumbai as if for an important assignment. But it was just to assist him with a draft proposal in HR division. I hope this time it may not be very different. I have a marriage to attend next week. My close friend after prolonged fight with parents has agreed to tie the knot. I prayed to God not to bother me with any unusual tasks.

The cabin crew has closed the door. The flight has taken off. I have time till I reach Mumbai. Normally, the race starts at 8 AM for me daily. Eye lids signal me to close the door. Naps at early morning flights are really enjoyable. I relish watching dreams. They are films without ticket. An online pass is available now.... The movie commences with display of names of actors and technical staff... Ehhh... This time it is a black and white screen... First time in my life.... Can I get French fries and a coke???

Night,13.08.1947, New Delhi- 4th floor of a vantage building.

A very dark room with one big candle in the middle of a table. Two Britishers are taking puffs. One of them releases a deep breath and looks at the other with cold eyes. A breeze is oozing out of the open windows. Slogans in Hindi and Bengali are heard from a distance.

John: It's all over, right?

Brenner: Yes, we are leaving but isn't it too early?

John: We have got enough return on investment and there is no point in continuing here. We have been freeing up all our colonies post the war. India has been our most profitable investment in last 2 centuries. Now the golden bird does not lay eggs (Laughs).

Brenner: But as far as I know, India can't be written off. One day, we will be held answerable.

John: India? Where is India? Do you have a map? The land of oracles and snake charmers. There is no nation called India. Once we leave, these baniyas will split into 500 fiefdoms. They will fight among themselves and die. How, do you think Brenner, that we captured this country of this size, larger than that of Britain, with so much of ease? It was Indians who facilitated us.

Brenner: Any way I am going to miss Sonakshi's and Kamala's (Laughs). Let me check if someone is available this night.

John: Hey, don't go out now. There is a pandemonium outside. These insane Indians are fighting. We may get caught and yes, we have an important visitor. He is waiting.

Brenner: Visitor? It is almost 12 PM.

John: He will interest you, Brenner. Just pick a bottle of wine and come back. We will have nice time.

Brenner goes out. John pulls the draw and takes one packet of cigar. Lighter kisses the stick. Smoke comes out hurriedly like a genie from a lost pot. John was reminiscing the day he landed in India. He was given charge of a taluka. Slowly he grew and became ruler of a presidency. This day, he sits at a bigger chair.... bigger than the whole country.

Through the open window, he sees a mob. Sickle with them is hungry for blood. A car sounding like a tractor enters the scene. Mob waylays it and pulls a man from the vehicle. Flames captures the scene. Huge cries.... Only man smiling in the surrounding is John.

A loud knock falls at his ears as an eye opener. A drop of water from the sky may be a curtain raiser. Rain may dance soon. How long can the clouds wait?

John: Yes, come in.

Two shades with black robes walks in, carrying bags of secrets with them. Are they from the same family? Future of INDIA is safe and secure in their coffers.

John: How could you reach here amid the din? I just saw a crowd burning a car.

Shade 1: Yes, it was our car.

John: How did you escape?

Shade 2: Great Indian rope trick (Laughs).

The table is full with bottles brought in by Brenner. Wine shines like the blood of Indians.

Brenner: John, you told the meeting is going to be interesting but this is inflammable.

John: You have brought lubricants, right? So, this will be more incendiary. Come on friends, let us open the wine for the prosperity of all.

The wine flows into 4 glasses followed by high cheering sounds in contrast to the shrieks all over the country.

Shade 1: We are at your service. We need your help till we get a foothold over India.

John and Brenner smiles at each other. The fox inside them speaks.

John: There is a bigger plan. We are not leaving India.

Brenner: What? Have not we packed our bags?

John lights another cigar. Smoke comes out with another story.

John: Calm down boy, I know, you are eager to meet Susan. That was a literary way of telling. Of course, we are leaving. We will continue to control Indians, their resource and the government.

John points at Shade 1: You have thousands of castes and languages. How will you manage this? If you listen to us, we will help you. You are not even a state with a proper governance structure. We will draft your laws, we will design your government, we will set your foreign policy… We will draw your school curriculum. You can't rule without us.

Shade 1: Yes, we need you. Big challenges are staring at us. We don't know to set them right.

John points at Shade 2: And you, always create tensions in India and Pakistan. You should spread British education here so that they are Indians in appearance and Britishers in thought.

Shade 2: That is what we have been doing.

John to Shade 1: But Mr. Shade, you will have a challenge. Ensure that Hindus and Muslims do not unite and always keep them in a boxing ring.

Shade 1 and Shade 2 converse in low tone to each other.

John: Is there an issue? Such a silly thing…Very easy to do. Both of them have burning thoughts.

Shade 2: Nothing. This plan will work.

John: Are you sure? Please open up. A minor error will sink all our heavy investments.

Shade 1(after a gap): Normally this is workable. I am apprehensive of only one gang which has the potential to be an irritant to us.

John: Who are those?

Shade 1: Leave it, Sir. We will take care of it. This won't last long.

John: We will crush every dissent. Money and muscle can buy anything. We will devise appropriate strategies at regular intervals. India will always be our colony. Let us disperse now. Sorry, we have to board the ship tomorrow.

Long stairs leading to first floor takes them to the library floor. Thoughts penned by thousands of scholars are sleeping inside, quite oblivious of the insidious design.

Bharath Mata Ki… Jai…Bharath Mata Ki…. Slogan that roars around the country….

Shade 1 flashes anxiety at his face. He uncovers his black robe. The man with white kurta, pants and a bald head looks like a good person. But he is a wise businessman, who sold his motherland and himself to the same ruthless traders who confined lakhs of his brothers to poverty.

Shade 2: What happened?

Shade 1: They are dangerous.... Really dangerous. They may derail our plan.

The Journalist in me says-

I am aghast at the game plan made by these foreigners. They preyed on us for years and nothing is left with us. We have to build a country from scratch. Decades back when these people landed at our bodies, we were a nation of prosperity. Our flags were flying high. Nobody could touch us. In 1947, majority of our population are living below poverty line. All major industries are ruined. Our life is in doldrums. On top of it, we have a religious fight to handle. We are sitting on fire and these people want to squeeze us again. What is left? This land is wet with tears and blood of our brothers and sisters. Many wives had never been fortunate enough to lead a family life. Many mothers met their child in death bed. Mother India has no jewels.

It is heart wrenching to note that few of my country men are also part of this plot. Their aim is to enslave Indians perpetually. They will decide who will be in power. Politicians in power may act like servants to princess.

Oh god, who will save us from this? Give us the power......

Content

Chapter - 1	1
Chapter - 2	10
Chapter - 3	17
Chapter - 4	22
Chapter - 5	29
Chapter - 6	36
Chapter - 7	42
Chapter - 8	47
Chapter - 9	52
Chapter - 10	57
Chapter - 11	62
Chapter - 12	68
Chapter - 13	73
Chapter - 14	78
Chapter - 15	84
Chapter - 16	90
Chapter - 17	96
Chapter - 18	103
Chapter - 19	109
Chapter - 20	114
Chapter - 21	122

Chapter - 1

The story is not regarding the deleterious game of Britishers…It will revolve around a small village in Tamil Nadu…If you are from Delhi, please take a flight to Madurai…From there another 50 kms by bus will take you to my place. I am among the group of people who live for my country. My sweat and tears are for my nation. My decision to pursue journalism after my graduation was staunchly opposed by my parents. They dreamt of me as a CA. Destiny wiped out all their complaints as they are happily reading my articles on papers.

Since, you have reached Madurai, before taking the bus, I would request you to get on to a time machine. We have to travel 50 years back to read this novel. You are on a bus run by coal. It will take 4 hours to travel 50 kms. The road on which we ride has a magic in itself. Bus moves very slowly. Cities and villages are going back to 1974. You may sleep for few minutes. I will call you as and when we have something special to see through the window.

Yes, get up. We have reached the village. It is going to rain heavily.

Ah…someone has put colors to the scene. This looks more attractive like movies of late 70s…. Let us enjoy this without any interval…I wish, if I get a recliner sofa and a set of beverages…. Since I don't carry an umbrella, we will have to drench…I don't mind it considering the excitement of walking on a village road.

01.07.1974, 5 AM.

We are in KALIKAPURAM-50 kms towards north of Madurai. The village is named after the famous, 5000-year-old KALI temple. Each drop in the large pond exactly in the middle of the sprawling 3-acre land has many stories to tell. The pond has no history of drying up. Village elders believe that goddess does not like to have fishes in the pond. The temple is the originating point of all tales of the village. An eerie silence pervades the village even on daytimes. People have often seen unknown ladies, in red sarees and holding a sickle, strolling on streets. They are considered to be messengers of KALI. The next day of their appearance, a criminal from the village will disappear. Police officers in Kalikapuram, are always in a relaxed state of mind. This area is clean of rape / domestic violence against women. As per a popular belief, any wrong doer will be imprisoned by Kali in the pond. Taking bath in the pond is considered to be a sin. Villagers treat the pond water as tears of Kannagi, an incarnation of devi, who lived in Madurai and finally dissolved at the feet of the mother.

Sound of incessant rain wakes up Parvathy. Unexpected rains are always auspicious for them. She sees Angaiathal on road with a big pot in her hand. Women have to walk a mile to fetch water. Promise of the Village Head to dig a well remains half baked. A big well, dug near to the house of Chettiar is the only source of water to the inhabitants. Ladies proposed a rain harvest system to be built in the locality…. In India, man proposes…politician disposes.

Chettiar migrated to this village from east. Elders say that he was made to flee from his village when his money lending business flopped. That man restarted his life as a servant in Nachaippan's house and one fine day, he became the land lord. Another set of people trust that Chettiar knows black magic and hence is respected and revered. Children have seen him sitting in grave yards and river banks. He does not visit temples except on festivals.

Parvathy: Angai, are you going to fetch water?

Angai: Yes, are you coming? Today being Amavasi, we need to go early.

Parvathy: Give me a second. I will just come.

She goes inside and comes back with a pot. Amavasi is the day when villagers gather at Kalika temple to pray for their well-being. Everybody has small dreams- a good home, road to travel and a cycle. On that day, they sacrifice a goat and share the precious meat. Today's goat is dedicated by Chettiar.

There was an announcement at the temple- A person who does not want to disclose his name has contributed a hen for the pooja today.

You may think why these ladies are going to fetch water from well when it is raining. There will be more such instances which you may find contrary…This is the land of riddles.

Parvathy was 16 when she got married to Nanda in 1930's, quite unaware of the British Raj and struggles in the country. For her, the village chief was the ruler of this earth. Being a quick learner, she picked up Sanskrit from a local scholar. In those days, girls were married off at 13 or 14. Family became increasingly worried as she nurtured the dream of going to Madurai for the graduation. ARYA SAMAJ agreed to take her to the city for higher studies. A first class in 10th STD implanted an atom bomb in the family. Unfortunately, she was sent to uncle's house which culminated in the marriage.

Nanda has 7 acres of farm land- partially ancestral. Feeding 7 kids with diverse interests has been a big challenge for him. He started with 2 acres and slowly expanded his empire.

Parvathy smiles at the red saree, the favorite present by Nanda. Saree covered her body with speed. Batter inside the pot is on the process of becoming a full-fledged idly.

Sita: Amma, it is time for school.

Parvathy: Two minutes, Sambar is on flames.

Nanda: Parvathy, when is the function at temple. Are you going to farm today?

Parvathy: No, I am not coming today, Whole day will be spent at the temple. After the pooja, nobody stays back for cleaning. Angai and I does it. Today, Angai may not come.

Sita: What happened to Angai akka?

Parvathy: She is going to her uncle's house for a marriage.

Nanda: So, you will be late today. Let me see if I can help you in the evening.

Sita: Amma, I will come to temple after school.

A village elder sounds the conch shell, marking the beginning of the pooja. Headcount is lesser than expected. Street vendors with flowers and toys are sitting in a line. River adjacent to the temple sings an old song... Priest takes holy dip in the river twice and opens the SREE KOVIL. Devi is very dark today. Has any asura taken birth somewhere?

People are dancing outside the temple, some in inebriated state. The goat tied nearby the temple does not know, that it is the last day on earth. A kid comes to the goat and feeds him. Kid is trying to play with the animal. Soon his mother comes and drags him back.

Priest is chanting slokas in Tamil. There are 4 juniors with different tasks like arranging flowers and beautifying the deity. Priest is usually very happy on Amavasi days. He gets lot of money but today his face is cloudy. After 2 hours of chanting, priest comes out. The troop sloganeers for KALIKA. Cries of the goat reaches the maximum. Finally, the time has come. Front side of the temple turns red.

Temple is closed for the day. There will be no afternoon and evening sessions. Meat is brought to kitchen. Parvathy and other village ladies start their work. It is announced that lunch will be served at 12 PM. Village elders gather below the banyan tree.

Lunch has mutton, chicken and salad as curries. Everybody is praising Parvathy for her preparation. Ladies are whispering that Kali won't be happy without Parvathy on new moon days.

Sita: I have been waiting for you since 5 PM.

Nanda: Yes, Parvathy, you need to rest now.

Parvathy: We will leave in 10 minutes.

The walk from temple to home takes around 10 minutes. Parvathy feels an ache in her legs. If Nanda and Sita had not come to help her, work would have got extended till 10 PM. Washing of utensils to cleaning of temple ground and disposal of waste is the responsibility of Parvathy and Angai.

The long day has left many marks on Parvathy. She was serving Kalika from 8 AM in the morning. As Angai was absent, she had to stretch to complete the day.

Nanda: One day, Kalikambal will pay you in lumpsum.

Parvathy smiles. She holds the hand of Sita.

Nanda: When can we walk on a good road? I have been seeing this mud road from childhood.

Sita: Let me become the collector, I will build a road for you, Appa.

Nanda: (Smiles) We should have taken a choola with us. See no lights on the road.

Parvathy: Be careful of dogs. They may be sleeping on the way.

Nanda: I am walking very slow.

Nanda stops for a while. There is a hill and a forest on his left side. The land is full of foxes and they howl 24/7. He holds Sita closely. The hill is called Narikunnu. Nobody enters that forest even during day light. It is ruled by dark forces. The only inhabitants are owls other than foxes. Once a journalist came to the village for a short stay. After hearing about the hill, he wanted to take pictures of it. Few of the leftist people also planned to accompany him. They approached the village head for the sanction. He denied it and informed them that if they go to Narikunnu, the entire village will see huge floods. A group of villagers locked the journalist and his company in a room. The very next day, villagers saw the broken lock of the room. Nobody has ever seen the gang in the village after that day. Heavy rain followed this-Village saw devastating floods.

Parvathy: Many people have seen Chettiar on this hill during nights.

Sita: Oh, we reached. Appa, I am not able to see anything. It is very dark.

Parvathy: Here is the key, Anna, you open the door.

Nanda goes towards the door…

Sita: Angai akka is still not back. Raghu mama has slept. Everyone else are in deep sleep other than us.

An owl is sitting on the mango tree. She makes a weird sound. Amavasi and owls….

The thought ship of Parvathy sails again. She is more worried about the mysteries surrounding her family than her financial plight. Right from birth, her children faced many hurdles in life…even those that could have ended their life. Somehow, last few years have been peaceful. She believes that Kali has been protecting them from all bad situations.

Nanda: Hey, who are you? – He asks someone.

Sita: What happened Appa?

Nanda: A person is sitting behind the mango tree. Who is he? Is it a male or female? A thief, a criminal or a beggar. Who are you?

Parvathy: Ayo, don't go near

It is a man. He gets up- a tall and well-built man. Long hair and shabby clothes and unshaven face makes him a beggar. The man comes near to Nanda. Parvathy and Sita cries in fear. There is no one around. The darkness of Amavasi becomes thicker. The light from the big sickle in his radiates all around. What is he up to? Foxes are howling at Narikunnu…

Who is he?

The Journalist- This is a village of mysteries. I have seen similar instances in my house. There were lot of oracles in this place till 5 years back. Kali Temple was their main meeting place. They earned a living by predicting future. Nobody knew where they slept or where they ate. I have seen them taking bath in temple pond. This is an act which others don't dare to do. They demanded very less money for the work. My father had great appreciation for them. Problems, small or large were handled by them in a very prescient manner. The gang had a chief who was believed to be 150 years old. My grandfather has been seeing him from his childhood. One day the chief died of heart attack.... Villagers have not seen any oracle after this. People murmur that the team has left the village.

Passenger next to my seat woke me up and I am welcomed by warm smile of air hostess. She enquired about my breakfast. I felt agitated and started sleeping again.

I think that the man holding the sickle may be an old oracle and he has come back for a reason. I felt afraid of cabin crew and prayed Kali to give me a good sleep.

Chapter - 2

Parvathy is an expert in cutting fruits within minutes. She has a sack full of fruits to work upon. Sita has been running around here for a while. Nanda along with his friends are dropping local wines from bottles. Kesav, Alagu and Ramesh have come. Their wives are helping Parvathy in the kitchen. The entire village is reduced to a single spot. Angai comes rushing to the scene with a great speed.

Nanda: Angai, why don't you try running in competitions. I am sure, you will win trophies.

Angai (gasping): I heard Narayan has come. I had to run from bus stop. The village head was talking to some people under the banyan tree. I overheard. Where is he?

Nanda: Go inside. Your Parvathy is making a big lunch for the entire village. Today is Pongal for us.

Angai could hear loud voices of Nanda and friends. She has not seen Nanda in happy mood after Narayan left the village.

The Journalist- I last met Narayan 6 years back. He was our school team captain for football. We all loved him for his strong passes. One day, I was told that he failed in 10th exam. After two years, he went off from the village.

Angai: Parvathy, yesterday it drizzled, right. This is the blessing of KALIKA.

Parvathy: Yes, Angai. Happiness has returned to our family. Devi saw my tears.

Angai: Where is he?

Parvathy: He came very late yesterday. He is in the second room. Don't know if he is sleeping. Just check.

Angai slowly moves to the room. She is carrying a pack of local sweet with her. She sees Narayan sleeping on the floor.

Angai to herself: Appa, 6 years has changed this boy. See his beard and he has lost lot of weight. Looks like a sanyasi now…

She keeps a pack in his room and goes back.

Angai: Parvathy, he is sleeping. I will go home, freshen up and come back soon.

Parvathy: Akka. You come fast. We have lot of work here.

Angai: I brought keera vadai for him. Ask him to eat it.

Parvathy sees Narayan lying on the floor. She touches his forehead. She feels a slight heat and takes her hand back. He is not feverish and how come the body is hot.

Parvathy: Narayan… Narayan… son.

The boy looks at his mother.

Narayan: Amma. Last night, were you afraid on seeing me? (Laughs)

Parvathy: Who will not be frightened seeing a figure like you on a new moon day? From a very young age, you have this habit of making drama. Where is that sickle that you were holding?

Narayan: That was the sickle of Raghu mama. I took it from his house.

Parvathy: Did you give it back? Raghu was complaining that his sickle is missing.

Narayan: It is kept outside. You can give it back.

Parvathy: Okay, now the barber will come. I want you to have a good haircut and shave. People will make fun of you, if they see you like this.

Narayan: Okay Amma, I will just come.

Narayan to himself: Why did I leave this beautiful village and my mother?

Cutting Narayan's hair is a tedious task. He has not had a cut during last 12 months. Beard has grown and is about to touch his heart. Achu is the sole man doing this job in the village. He has been seeing Narayan since childhood. Narayan was a boy loved and cared by all in the area.

Nanda: I still remember the day, he was born. It was raining heavily. It was not a rainy season. We had severe drought in the preceding month.

Raghu: We were in our ancestral village when this incident happened. I came to know about this after I returned.

Nanda: I have never seen Nachiar after that night.

3 people are sitting beside Nanda and hearing his anecdote. A cool, breeze fills the air.

A friend: Have you asked him where he has been all these years?

Nanda: He just reached. We will talk in detail.

Friend: Give him some time to relax.

Nanda: On that rainy day, village was sinking and we shifted to the hill. A makeshift tent was made for our stay. I still wonder, not a single fox was seen on that hill. It was Nachiar who suggested us to go to the hill as water will not reach there.

Narikunnu is a hill inhabited by foxes. Talks are that the place has no end. Rationalists believe that the hill is a home to precious minerals. There are industrialists from Madras taking benefits. Blind faith tells that people who die early in their life take rebirth as foxes in the hill and keeps on howling....

Friend: Nachiar was a great astrologer and Karmi.

Nanda: Then the labor pain started. We were expecting it to happen next week. There was no chance of cessation of rain. I did not know what to do. We were not having a single woman who could do this.

Friend: Water reached Makudam of KALIKA temple. We lost all hope.

Nanda: Then Nachiar sat below one tree and started to chant mantras. Time was passing soon and cries of Parvathy became louder. Along with her, other ladies also started crying. I went to Nachiar and held his feet. After few minutes, the baby was born. What was the magic behind that? I got the information that it is a baby boy. Immediately, Nachiar prepared his horoscope and gave to me. He predicted that my son will become a famous person.

Friend: Next day rain stopped. We all returned to homes. We don't know which mantras saved Parvathy?

Nanda: In that joy, we forgot Nachiar. I searched everywhere to thank him. Nachiar's family gave compliant to Police. The entire village went on a search mission. On the 3rd day, when we were walking near by the hill, we could smell a stench. We also saw a fox moving to woods with a piece of flesh. Nobody had the courage to go up and check. I decided to go inside and it started to rain again. My leg was stuck somewhere. Oh. It was Nachiar…. Half of the body was eaten by foxes.

Nanda and friends are in silence. Reels are going on in their minds.

Friend: May Nachiar dissolve at HER feet.

Nanda is in tears. He drinks a cup of water and reclines on a chair.

Friend: Do you know Nanda, Nachiar's son became a good astrologer now. He also does poojas.

Nanda: I have seen him but I don't go to astrologers now.

Achu comes inside the compound. He greets all of them.

Nanda: Hey, you were cutting my son's hair. Is it over?

Achu: What Anna, you have drunk a lot. Are you joking? I have just come from Chettiar's house. Ranga told me that Narayan has come back and I need to cut his hair.

Nanda: Arey, you came half an hour back and took my son to the backyard for cutting.

Achu: No Anna, I am just coming.

Parvathy comes out and sees Achu.

Parvathy: Achu, you are here. Then who is cutting the hair of Narayan?

Nanda shivers in fear. He gets up and runs to the back of the house. Friends pick up sticks and runs behind him. Achu and Parvathy goes inside the house and opens the back door.

They could not believe it. Are our eyes cheating us?

The Journalist- I have serious doubt about this episode. Achu is the sole barber in the locality. He knows each and every house. According to Nanda and Parvathy, Achu started his work half an hour back. They had seen him with their own eyes. Now another person with similar appearance has come. Though oracles had left this place few years back, we have people with knowledge of black magic here. My grandfather has been a repository of black magic stories. Some magicians have the power of changing their appearance. Others can take the shape of animals. There are people who can fly. Nanda and his family have been a victim of sorcery from early days. They fell at the feet of Kali Ma based on the advice of Nachiar. Prior to that, Nanda was an atheist. After dipping into bhakti, Nanda has not seen any miseries related to this. Breaking the fence of the dark world needs courage and Nanda has it.

Having said this, Achu is a person who likes to play prank. He was very close to Narayan from school days. They were notorious in making fun. My mind is oscillating between fantasy and reality.

Chapter - 3

Parvathy is washing utensils. The team of visitors have left. Only family members are chatting in the house. Nanda and sons are sitting in the compound. Ladies have gathered in a room. They are talking about inauguration of a new jewel shop on the next day. A famous actress is expected for the event. Parvathy is in the last lap of her work. She feels dry up after receiving the crowd and serving them the food.

Nanda: Parvathy, come here.

Parvathy: Will come in 2 minutes.

Parvathy washes her hands and appears in courtyard. There is a wave of tension in the face of Nanda and others. Parvathy to make things lighter……

Parvathy: Narayan, there is one person who has been waiting for your return.

Narayan: Who is it? (smiles).

Parvathy: Do you think, nobody knows about this? I had doubt from the beginning.

Narayan: Amma, I am bad at cracking puzzles.

Nanda: Parvathy, we will speak about it later… now I want to discuss something.

An air of stress comes from the nose of Nanda. It is a very cool night but Nanda is sweating. Birds are shifting back to their nests. The owl has marked it attendance. The night is slowly acquiring the silence. Nanda suddenly saw a car passing in front of his house. It is Chettiar. He usually hits the nest early. May be he had gone to a faraway place

Nanda: Narayan, tell me who cut the hair if it was not Achu?

Narayan: Appa, Achu might be playing a prank. He only cut my hair. He took Rs 10 extra from me.

Nanda: Narayan, stop this game. Achu reached after you had your cut.

Narayan: I don't know Appa. He might have come to you after exiting from backdoor.

Paravathy: I also saw Narayan going along with Achu for haircut. Kali, are you testing us again.

Other ladies in the house joins the discussion. They remain clueless as they were not witness to the event. Their mind is full of opening of first jewel shop in the village. They may not sleep for next two days due to the excitement of meeting the actress.

Parvathy: Anyway, let us not think too much on this. Who knows, if it is not the game of Achu. He likes making fun with us.

Ram (1st son): Tomorrow, I have to go to Madurai to get seeds. I am leaving (signals his wife to come with him along with kids). Narayan, hope you met your sister-in-law. She is Alli- daughter of Muthuraman.

Narayan: Yes, yes, I spoke to all. Why did I left this village? I missed all your marriages and other functions.

Nanda: Don't worry, we will get Sita married the next day so that you can also participate (everyone laughs).

Sita: Let me become the district collector and we will think of it.

Ravi (2nd son): Narayan, I heard that she likes someone from her school.

Narayan: Then we will get her married tomorrow itself (everyone laughs).

Sita: You are 23 now. Right time for marriage and I know Tamil akka is waiting for you.

Narayan: Podi… go inside (again laughs).

An anxiety hides behind the laughter of Nanda.

Parvathy: Okay, it is time to sleep. The village has slept. Let us go. Narayan, your old room is waiting for you.

Narayan's old bed is still there. Nobody used his room during his absence. The room still has the old smell. He looks at the roof. Through a tiny opening, he can see the sky. He liked watching the sky when he was young. His ambition was to travel to the sky. He told Parvathy once that he aims to make one aircraft by selling his cycle. The Head Master advised him about some colleges in Delhi and Bombay that teaches aviation. He planned to join those colleges but life was to take a different turn…

Narayan is recollecting the episode of haircut. He was exactly like Achu. For a moment, he saw Achu coming from the front gate and another Achu who was doing the cut. Next moment, the fake Achu vanished. He completed the haircut, took money and disappeared. Who was he? And for the astonishment, there was no single hair lying on the ground…… fairy-tale…

Narayan to himself: Are the stories repeating? - Nanda with a very low voice.

Doors are open. Today there are feeling unusual frost outside.

Nanda: Parvathy, you need not worry. This is a simple incident. Have not we seen more fiery things?

Parvathy: Why are they behind us? Who are behind our sons? I was happy when Narayan was away as he is safe.

Nanda: Nothing will happen. Kali will take care of our kids. Do you remember? Once an elephant ran amok in front of our house. What happened then? Kali saved us.

Parvathy: But why is this? Why should we live like this, in unending fear? What sin did we do?

Nanda: Tomorrow we will go to the son of Nachiar. I have been meeting him often. Nachiar was a powerful man and my guide. Son is also doing poojas now.

Parvathy: We will go on Wednesday. We have work at temple tomorrow.

Nanda hears huge noise of a crowd outside. People are running towards north. Is someone knocking at the door?

Nanda: Who can it be? What is the time now?

Nanda lights the lamp. Sita, Narayan, and Parvathy are behind him. It is dusty outside. When the dust settles, they see Raghu.

Nanda: Raghu, what happened?

Raghu takes time to control the gasp. Somehow, he explains the situation. A slight shiver passes through the body of Nanda. Parvathy stands frozen. Sita could not believe her ears. Narayan sits on the ground. The game starts.

The Journalist- For me Narayan was always a newsmaker. From his childhood, he has been in the limelight. His marks and achievements in exams were admired by all. News of his failure in the SSLC exam was a shock to all of us. In school games, he would score well but when it comes to finals, the results were different. Nobody would match his practice, fitness and his dedication. He version for all -his hits and misses hogged the headlines of local gossip makers. I never spoke bad about him but had been hearing extra ordinary things about him. Love story with Tamil flashes like an action-packed movie with thrills, horrors, stunts and suspense. Let me get exact details of it for the narrative.

Raghu, an old inhabitant is a carpenter. Nanda believes Raghu the most because of his virtues and ardent devotion to Kali Ma. Everyone calls him Anna, respectfully.

My question to nature is something different. Narayan has just touched the sand of this village and cinematic scenes are inserted into his life. Nature is the director of all life stories. What is in store for Narayan?

Chapter - 4

Friends have encircled Narayan. One of their friends have become constable in TN police. Ashok aspired of becoming a police from childhood. Villagers went on a celebration when he cleared exams and interview, as he was the first man to get into government services from that village. His mother brought him up by working in the farms after she lost her husband. She succumbed to a snake bite on the day Ashok got his first salary.

Ashok: The new SI is very adamant. You are a suspect. SI has not completely believed us.

Narayan: Story tellers have created numerous tales about the animosity between me and Chettiar. That might be the reason why SI is not trusting me.

Ashok: Who testified against you?

Narayan: I have never seen him in the village.

Narayan recollected Raghu's words: Someone has set fire to Chettiar's shop and it has burnt completely... As per a witness, Narayan is the culprit.

Ashok: All were very excited to attend the inauguration. Now this will become a talking point.

Another friend: The witness may be Chettiar's man. There was an issue between Chettiar and you.

Second Friend: Narayan, you be careful. You should not get into an issue with Chettiar now. He is not old Chettiar. He knows dark poojas.

Third Friend: Hey, how long will we remain afraid of him. We will cut his throat.

Narayan's mind is awash with thoughts. SI released Narayan based on the request of Ashok but on the condition that he will cooperate with the investigation. Raghu submitted that he was with Narayan till 11 PM and the incident happened at 10:30 pm. Narayan goes behind a video trailer of the past.

The question remains- Who is the culprit? From where did the witness come from?

Clock shows the time as 8 PM. The needles are very lazy this day. Parvathy places a plate of chips in the middle of the crowd.

Parvathy: Who all will be there for dinner?

Ashok: All will be here aunty. We got our friend back, right? You would have prayed at least 1000 times to Kali Ma for him, know?

Parvathy: Ashok, I am worried. Chettiar has lost huge money. Will he sit idle? He is a snake.

Ashok: Nothing will happen aunty, we are here. You go inside and prepare for dinner.

The owl makes the same sound, sitting on the mango tree. Parvathy sees Raghu and Nanda smoking behind the woods. Raghu picks up one beedi and gives to Nanda.

Nanda: Narayan, you be careful. Where ever you go, please take your friends along with you.

Narayan: Appa, I have not stepped outside the house.

Nanda: I know Narayan, I am telling you to be vigilant. You have spent just one day in this village and now see the drama. First Achu and now the Chettiar's shop.

Narayan: I am not guilty. Raghu mama, you tell me what have I done?

Raghu: There is no mistake on your side. We are advising you to be cautious. You might not have forgotten old stories. After you left, Chettiar made our life miserable. Recently he calmed down. He started helping us.

Narayan: If I leave this village again, will the problem be solved.

Nanda is thunderstruck after hearing this. Raghu looks at Nanda.

Nanda: We are planning to arrange a compromise with Chettiar. Let us see if it will work.

Parvathy after hearing this: Let us all have dinner now. We will discuss later. Today I have prepared special curries.

Narayan feels sleepy after the sumptuous dinner. The kerosene light is very dim. He puts it off and closes his eyes. His mind is wandering in the past.

Narayan was a brilliant boy in school. Everyone liked him for his disciplined learning and extra curriculars. He never opened his books at home. Studies were concluded at the classroom itself. Evenings were used for games and temple activities.

Narayan had big dreams of becoming a college lecturer. He wanted to do graduation in history. He was the most liked student in social science classes. He was also a regular visitor to the school library.

Journalist-How many dreams did he have? College lecturer, scientist.... IAS officer...

Everything was fine until that day...Sleep knocks at the door of Nanda... But when he opens, it vanishes.

Parvathy: That was the beginning of all.

A May month... Nanda felt back pain after heavy work at the field. Margins in the rice business is on a downfall. He did not know what to sow next. He could not drop rice as that was against his ethos. Lunch in the box lost patience as its karma was delayed. Nanda saw school head master coming towards him. This is an extraordinary instance...

Head Master: Hello Nanda, Is it not the time for food?

Nanda: Yes, yes, I was about to. Hope you are on leave today.

HM: I am not... I came to meet you. Today we did not have work at school.

Nanda: Is there anything urgent?

HM: How is Narayan doing at home? Does he spend time on his studies?

Nanda: He studies only at school but he scores well, right?

HM: Nanda, can we go to your home and talk I want to speak to Parvathy also.

Nanda and Parvathy had no clue of the words falling on their ears. The thin between truth and lie faded quickly.

Parvathy: Sir, please help. I want my son back.

HM: What can I do. Parvathy? He has not answered any question. How can we make him pass 9th standard. I am not able to understand how this happened? He has been topping the class till Christmas exams. I wonder how you people did not notice the change.

Parvathy: We were not aware of this?

HM: Shocking to see zero marks for Narayan. How can I send him to next class?

Nanda fell at the feet of HM. Tears made it wet.

HM: Nanda, get up. We will see what to do? Where is Narayan?

Parvathy (also weeping): He might be in the temple.

HM: Come on, let us go and talk to him.

Sun was very angry that day. He was waiting for his duty to get over and take a bath in the sea. Nanda was over confident that Narayan will score well in his exams. These days, Narayan was always in the temple or nearby forests. Nanda heard that, Narayan once went to Madurai to watch a film. Raghu told him about this but Nanda never asked.

Nanda saw the closed door of the temple.

HM: Noone is there in the temple. Where is he?

Nanda: He should be here.

Soon, a big sound…they saw two people coming from the temple. Seeing Nanda and HM, they ran away.

HM: Hey, guys… stop. Where is Narayan?

Nanda: Narayan… Narayan…. Narayan.

Narayan is not seen anywhere….an old Tamil song is played in the air…a dusty wind wandered in the temple. A sound of conch shell, a loud laughter, beating of a dholak and at last cry of an owl…. Two crows fly out of a nearby tree. The clouds started making noise in the sky. Sun became black.

HM: Nanda, something is wrong. We should leave now.

Nanda: Narayan, Narayan…where are you?

The Journalist- Did you notice the owl sitting on the Mango tree. Owl is considered to be a messenger in this village. The news can be a bad one or a good one. People believe that, if owl visits your village and stays there for a long time, it is your turn to receive the news. An owl has conquered mango tree of Nanda's house since last week. This has brought good news to him- Narayan has come back. But immediately after his return, problems have started to crop up in his family. There was a friction between Chettiar and Narayan few years back. You will come to know the reason later. Now his new shop is burnt and there is a witness against our hero. Is this again a magical story or the truth is yet to be seen.

This night, Nanda is disturbed- how his dreams about Narayan shattered and how his course of life changed and so on.

I have only one statement to make- Man proposes…God disposes.

Chapter - 5

Nanda and Parvathy finds it difficult to circumvent their feelings. Old stories have become a big sea around them. Their small yacht may not be insulated from the inclement weather.

Nanda: HM helped us. He gave a second chance to Narayan. Someone else would not have done that.

Parvathy: HM expected a first class in 10th. HM was a pious man. That was the first instance of flouting of rules by him.

Nanda: But the issue was not to end. HM helped us in 9th but what could have he done in 10th?

Parvathy: The village was ambitious of Narayan.

Nanda: What was Narayan doing in the temple on that day? After the storm, we saw him lying on the ground. We did not tell you Parvathy, he was drunk.

Parvathy: What? Does he have that habit even now?

Nanda: Let us keep our hopes alive.

Parvathy: Kali ma, what is my son up to? Is this the reason why you gave us four sons. Please protect them.

Nanda: HM was closely following up Narayan from day 1 of 10th class. He regularly conducted class tests. I am ashamed that our son was hiding his real character. Narayan failed to appreciate the efforts of HM.

Parvathy: My son is good. It was the game of planets.

Nanda: There is no use lamenting now. Still, he has time.

Parvathy: He has not passed 10th.

Nanda: I have spoken to the current head master. He will allow Narayan to write the exam through self-study. Sita can help.

Parvathy: I don't know. You speak to Narayan tomorrow.

Nanda: My son did not reappear for 10th exam. After the results, HM was devastated. He hoped Narayan will redo and pass the exam.

Parvathy: We saw a different Narayan for the next 3 years.

Nanda: Bairava took him to Madurai for a job and spoiled my child. He declined my advice to join the farm. He started sleeping at Bairava's home whenever he came to our village. He was a bhakt of Kali Ma. Slowly he stopped going to temple.

Parvathy: Not a single day passed without going to temple during his childhood. He fasted on every new moon day.

Nanda: I don't think that fight with Chettiar was the reason behind his departure.

Parvathy: I don't know. Tomorrow we should meet Nachiar's son. What is happening around?

Nanda: You have his horoscope in our old almirah. We will go tomorrow.

Nanda gets up at 5 AM. Snores of Parvathy are hitting the roof. Nanda closes his eyes. He did not sleep well yesterday. It is cold outside. He can hear chirps of birds on the trees. Again, a wave of thoughts washes his shore. What could be the future of Narayan? The other three are well settled now. They are living in their own houses and have a good family life. All girls are married and are living happily. Sita is studying well and is likely to get a first class in 10th exam. The only sadness is around Narayan. How long can Nanda sustain him? Nanda is getting old. Ram has promised to take over Nanda's farm and relieve him. Nanda is planning for his retirement. He has instructed his three sons to take care of Sita.

Nanda: Parvathy, sun will rise now. We will go to temple first and then to the house of Nachiar.

Parvathy: What do you want for breakfast?

Nanda: We will eat after coming back. Ask Sita to prepare food. Nachiar's son will be very busy after 10 AM. We should meet him before that.

Parvathy: Ok. I will come in 10 minutes.

She goes out to take bath. Nanda looks at the owl sitting on the mango tree. What is the owl doing here? It first appeared when he was planning for a trip to Neermalai temple. Neermalai is a nearby village and it has a famous temple of Muruga. Nanda visits that temple whenever he feels sad. Owl is considered to be an omen in the village. Owl's lives in Narikunnu and comes out only when they have to tell anything to a family. It is considered that if an owl appears in a house, then something important will happen in that place within next one month, whether it is bad or good, only time will tell.

The owl can leave now… The news is delivered…

The Journalist- I told you about the owl earlier…

Parvathy: Anna, please come soon.

Parvathy calls in a loud voice…. Shriek…. Nanda rushes inside…Temperature of Parvathy has fell below 0 degree.

Nanda: What happened?

Parvathy: Horoscope is missing.

Nanda: What? Did we search properly.

Parvathy: It was inside this almirah. I saw it yesterday. N

Nanda searches the desk... There are few books and sarees. He takes it out and checks. He gets a red color cloth. He opens it and sees a paper.

Nanda: See, this is the one, you have been scouting for.

Parvathy: I kept it in that book. Who moved it to the cloth. Red stripe was kept for temple functions.

Nanda opens the paper. A fear grips his face. Weight of his hands drops down. The paper falls from his arms. A small golden snake sneaks out. It raises the head and looks at Narayan. Suddenly it dies……

Narayan: What is it, Appa?

Nanda: I don't know, son? I feel something is going to happen.

Parvathy: Come immediately we have to reach Nachiar's house.

Parvathy and Nanda have to walk 10 minutes to go to that place. There is a govt bus at 7:30 AM from the next bus stop. But they may miss it. If they walk fast, they can touch the destination by 8 AM. Muthu, Nachiar's son will be free by that time. Raghu said that Muthu gets up by 4 AM in the morning, does his poojas and sits for consultation by 8:30 AM. Nanda has long relationship with the family of Nachiar.

Nanda: Muthu will be having breakfast when we arrive at the house. We will get good time to talk to him before people come. I have seen Muthu in child clothes.

Parvathy: Muthu has blessings of Kali Ma. I heard Police sought his advice in shop burning case and he confirmed that it was not done by our son. SI is a regular customer of Muthu. Now people are calling him Swamy ji.

They are about to reach Muthu's house. Nobody is seen in the compound. Nanda opens the gate.

Parvathy: Ahh…

A crow comes and sits on her head for a second and flies away.

Parvathy: I am afraid. Will Muthu predict something bad.

Muthu comes out with a smile. He has few flowers in his hand. He gives it to Parvathy. She takes it with a reply smile.

Muthu: What happened Nanda uncle? You look worried. Is everything ok?

Nanda: Yes, my mind is full of doubts. I am anxious. You would have heard that Narayan is back to village. Unexpected events are happening after that. We need your help. I am eager to know about his future.

Muthu: What do you want to know?

Nanda: I have his chart. You know the issues which he has been creating since his 9th standard. At last, he left the village. Now he has come back after 6 years. We have not asked him about his past till now. How will he live here without getting a job. He does not know farming. Above all lot of furtive things are happening.

Muthu: Show me his horoscope.

Nanda hands it over to Muthu.

Soon astonishment covers his face. His eyes are oscillating between Parvathy and Nanda. He is not able to move his lips for some time. With closed eyes, he chants some mantras. Parvathy is afraid that Muthu will make an adverse prediction. A lizard falls from the ceiling on Nanda. Muthu opens his eyes and sees a dog running behind a hen. Dogs captures the hen and blood oozes out. Screams of the prey fills the atmosphere. Howling of the foxes reaches the peak.

The Journalist- Being a rationalist, I don't personally believe in astrology. How can planets located miles away affect your fortune? Recently, I met an expert in the field who briefed me about fundamentals of the subject. He convinced me that there are powers in the nature that control your life.

Astrology is a method developed by gods to help man when he is in wilderness. I am empathetic towards Nanda and Parvathy as parents of Narayan. Yes, let Muthu guide them to solve the problem.

Chapter - 6

How can a chart prepared by Nachiar be wrong? Muthu looked at it again and again. The conundrum has multiple dimensions. His eyes immersed into disquiet. Popularity of Nachiar broke all directions. Even after 23 years of bereavement, he stands first among renowned astrologers in 25 km circle.

"Oh God- give my father back for a moment…. This error can hurt the goodwill created by him… What should I say to these anxious parents?" … Ecstasy gives way to dilemma.

His father once told Muthu that he only tells people what Kali tells him. Bad dreams had been Muthu's regular visitor since last full moon day. His aura could negative smell energy from the horoscope-Yes, this a chart with errors.

Muthu: Uncle, this chart needs inspection by a higher authority. My knowledge has limitations.

Nanda: Is there any problem?

Muthu: Nothing, we face such situations…. mind becomes blank. I want presence of my guru here.

Nanda: Is everything ok, Muthu?

Muthu: There are powers beyond the comprehension of human mind. I am sure that they will protect us.

Eyes of Muthu is fixed at the sky. The answer has to come from there. He picks up one yantra and hands it over to Nanda.

Muthu: Ask Narayan to wear this. He should take dip at the temple pond every day and pray to Kali Ma. He should not move out of the house after 7 PM. Don't worry, nothing will happen when he baths in the pond.

Nanda: When should I come back?

Muthu: I will check with my guru. He is in Madurai. I will come to your home in 21 days.

Muthu hands over another 4 yantras.

Muthu: Please make 4 digs at four corners of your house and deposit each one of this yantra. This should be done in the evening.

Muthu gives a red-colored bag to Nanda. He keeps all yantras in the bag.

Muthu: Ramu, please take my bullock cart and drop them at their house. Please chant Aswaroooda before starting the journey. Avoid Narikunnu. It may take a bit longer to reach but do that.

Nanda: No Muthu. We will walk.

Muthu (in a strong voice): Uncle, please listen to my instructions for the next 21 days. Ramu, please drop them.

Muthu calls his wife Suganthi. She comes with a jug of water.

Muthu: Suganthi, I am going to sleep. Please do not disturb. I will get up only in the evening. No poojas today.

A 90-year-old man with black hair will come by 6 PM. Take him to pooja room then.

The wheels of the cart are familiar to this road but today there are hesitant to roll. Is it because they are asked to cover more distance?. Ramu has no clue regarding the case but he saw Muthu in doldrums. What happened to him? Ramu, the best student has been with Muthu since childhood. He has never seen Muthu in a poser. Muthu is always strong and calculative. Muthu lost his father, Nachiar at an early stage. His grandfather relocated from Madurai to this village post that. Grand Father was also a great astrologer and priest. He trained Muthu in tantra for 12 years. One day morning grandfather called Muthu and gave him some mantras and left the village. Before parting ways, the old man advised Muthu to go to Madurai and learn poojas under a guru. Muthu came back after 3 years and since then he is an umbrella and a peepal tree. It is believed that the Kali comes to meet Muthu every midnight.

Muthu never wanted to marry. One day evening, a girl by name Suganthi asked Muthu to marry her. Her eyes were red. Muthu sought permission of Kalika for this. The marriage happened the very next day. Some people say that Suganthi is one of the Yakshinis of Kali and she is making predictions on behalf of Muthu.

One day, water in the temple pond turned red. Ashes were also seen in the pond. Nobody knew, how a fire could happen inside the pond. First time, people were seeing water on fire. Devotees turned to Muthu for help. After hearing this, Muthu went to Chettiar's house along with a group of people. He spoke to Chettiar in a closed room.

Both of them came out and went to the pond. Chettiar stood on the west side and Muthu on the east. They meditated for some time and later pond became normal.

Ramu: First time, I am seeing Muthu Anna like this. Whose chart did you show him?

Nanda and Parvathy woke up. The cart is comfortable with good cushions and curtains. Anyone can travel 50-100 kms with ease. They rarely travel in carts. Either they walk or go by bus. Both of them have never used a motor car. Shyam, the third son is doing business and is planning to buy a car. He has promised family trips after that.

Nanda: My son's.

Ramu: Don't worry, the chart may be so good that Muthu Anna needs to consult his guru.

Nanda: Hope so.

Ramu: Since we are taking a deviation to avoid Narikunnu, we will be late.

Nanda: That is fine, I am not going to work.

Ramu: Anna, what is your son doing?

Nanda: He has just come back after a world tour (Nanda is laughing).

Ramu: Your life will change. Muthu Anna will guide you.

Bulls have started showing signs of tiredness. It took 2 hours to cover the distance. Since Narikunnu was to be evaded, Ramu drove 10 kms extra.

"Shiva and Krishna…. You both have become very lazy these days" …. Ramu to bulls.

Nanda takes Rs 10 from the pocket.

Ramu: No, I won't take money. Can I meet your son? Muthu Anna told to see him and come.

Nanda: Come inside.

Ramu: No, instruction is not to enter your house. I have to see him at a distance and go back. Please call him.

Nanda is surprised. He goes inside and calls Narayan. Sita is ready to go to school.

Sita: What Appa, why are you late? You know exams are fast approaching. I should not miss classes.

Nanda: Where is he, Narayan?

Nanda is gasping for breath. His words emanate fear.

Nanda: Parvathy, where is Narayan?

Sita: He has gone out with an old friend.

Nanda: Narayan is not here. Please drink a glass of water.

Ramu: No, it is ok, I will come later.

The cart goes ahead slowly with a sound. Ramu with his imagination makes the picture of Narayan. He draws and redraws it. After the first turn, he sees a tall man with a neatly cut hair and white complexion.

I have seen him before. No, it may be wrong. There are 7 people with similar faces in this world. God does the magic.

Ramu is perplexed. Is it the same person?

Yes, it is the same person. He was fat when I met him. He knows me well.

The tall man looks at Ramu and walks past him.

Ramu to himself: He is not recognizing me. Is he the same guy.

Ramu stops the cart by side and gets down. He walks behind the tall man. The tall man enters Nanda's house.

Ramu: Is he Narayan? If he is Narayan, it is not the person whom I Know or are both of them same?

Events which happened 2 years back starts to unfold in Ramu's mind.

Ma Kali… Ramu exasperates.

Journalist-I understand that this may be annoying. A great person like Nachiar had written the horoscope and how can it go wrong? My assumption is that he prepared the chart in a hurry and missed many things. Nachiar made the horoscope on the day of birth itself and within minutes. Nachiar passed away immediately after that. A simple error has caused so much agony to Nanda.

Narayan is back home now and what might be his plans. He has spent less than a week here and I am eager to know his future. Such a talented man cannot waste his life. I wish to see his energy and resource in action. Only time has the answer for this.

Ramu has never gone out of this village. He joined Muthu few years back. He has never met Narayan. Devi, this dream is dragging me to the end of this universe.

Chapter - 7

Narayan sees fire in the eyes of Nanda. He searched for water to put it off.

Nanda: Didn't I tell you not to walk alone? You have come to the place after 6 years. The village has changed. New people have come in.

Narayan: I went to see one of my close friends.

Nanda: Ok come inside and drink water. I need to talk to you in detail.

Narayan: Let me take a bath and come.

Temperatures are hitting the sky. Narayan is meeting Sreedhar after 10 years. He did intermediate from a posh college in Madras. Sreedhar was an average student in all subjects except science and was ambitious of becoming a space scientist. His Uncle, a very influential businessman, got him an admission in MCC. Life worked like a conjurer for Sreedhar. After scoring a first class in intermediate and B Sc Physics, he landed in ISRO as a scientist. He wishes to marry Tamil. Sreedhar is unaware of his relation with her, he requested Narayan to speak to her.

Narayan's relationship started in 8th class. Narayan was afraid to tell regarding their affair to anyone. Fater passing 10th exam with a second class, Tamil did BA in English and is teaching in a school nearby. When Narayan left the village, he dropped a letter in her house. It was to instruct her not to wait for him. Narayan still does not know if she received the letter. From Sreedhar he learnt that she is still unmarried. Was she waiting for him? A girl not getting married at the age of 23 is a sin in this village.

Nanda: Why did you leave this place? Where were you all these days?

10 days has passed after Narayan's arrival. He was expecting this question from Parvathy first. That may be out of curiosity or concern. It is true that there were some altercations with Chettiar and team during the temple festival and Narayan's friend stabbed one of the opponents but that was not the exact reason for his exodus.

Next moment, Nanda and Parvathy see Narayan weeping for the first time in their life. Is it the same Narayan, 6 feet tall man with a 56-inch chest, who is weeping? Nanda and Parvathy could not stand by it. Parvathy carries Narayan in her arms.

Narayan: Amma, nobody believes me.

Parvathy: Let the whole world stand against you. I will be with you.

Narayan: I lost control of my life. It was not me who failed in 10th class. I knew answers for all questions but someone was holding me back from writing.

Parvathy: Forget it. You tell me why you left the village and where you were?

Nanda is also in tears. He is very disturbed after visiting Muthu. Nanda's last hope revolves around Muthu.

Narayan: I need to meet a doctor. I am not able to recollect anything. I remember going to Madurai after my failure in 10th.

Parvathy: Anna, we should meet the doctor today itself. My kid is in problem. He was a bright child at school. See now, he is in shambles. Where should we go?

Nanda: I think our Chinna Vaidyar will help us.

Parvathy: No, we should go to Madurai and check his whole body. We should treat every bad energy in him.

Nanda: First let us consult the Vaidyar and later we will go to Madurai.

Parvathy: Ok. Let him take rest now. I will tie the yantra given by Muthu. We will do a special pooja at Kali temple during next Amavasi. Narayan, you take rest now. Tomorrow we will go to Vaidyar.

Tamil is working with a secondary school in a town. Half saree gave way to full-fledged saree. She talks like a teacher. Her scores for English were abysmally poor at school. Don't know how she became an English teacher. She once said that she likes to remain unmarried and get into politics.

Tamil was brought up by her uncle. Father had been working in Tenkasi. Mother made money by running a diary. They had small dreams about Tamil. Kali Ma gave Tamil to her parents after 6 years of marriage. Tamil learnt all poojas and mantras of the temple. She missed her school during Amavasi days. Once she even decided to skip her exams for the temple festival. Her uncle, a politician. wanted Tamil to marry his son. Uncle predicted a bright future for Tamil in politics and asked her to join youth wing of his party, which she politely denied. Narayan hated her uncle. He was always carrying a pistol with him.

Tamil: I am alone. My mother passed away 3 years back in a bus accident, on her way back from Palani. I rarely come to the village. I got the news of your return from Angai. She writes to me every month.

Narayan: Tamil, I am sorry for your mother.

Tamil: Life has changed a lot. Uncle became MLA. In next election he will be a minister. His son married the daughter of Chettiar. Uncle made preparations for my marriage with Senthil but I backed off. Uncle does not talk to me.

Narayan: Did not you get my letter which I dropped in your house before my travel.

Tamil: I got it but I could not forget you. Why did you go from here? I have been crying all these years.

Narayan: Tamil, I want to tell you something. Life is not easy. I am jobless. I have no money. I can't predict where my life will move. So....

Tamil: So, What? What you want to tell.

Narayan sees 2 Tamils- 1 girl with all happiness in life, a deluxe living without worries and another Tamil, the wife of Narayan with a broken dream.

Narayan loses control of his tongue. An invisible force captures him and makes him say what he did not wish to.

Narayan: Be ready for uncertainties after our marriage.

A loud laughter comes out of her throat. It is the best day of her life. She has been waiting for this and today she in heaven. Tamil hugs Narayan and kisses him on his cheek.

Narayan to himself: What have I done?

Behind the laughter and noises, Narayan sees a man with a sad face standing near the coconut tree… It is Sreedhar.

Journalist-I am so tired and it will be unfair if I indulge in your imagination. So, I request you people to kindly use your own creative faculties to do this journey. I would join you back after sometime. Let me sleep and continue my dream…. Hope the airhostess has no plans to treat me with a cup of coffee.

Chapter - 8

Muthu has a big light with him but the fire seems to be dim. Ramu is preparing for a pooja asper guidance of guru. Today is the deadline to complete the ritual. This is an auspicious day to complete the task. Ramu brings a pot full of water and red flowers. He draws a big chart in the pooja room. Guru will offer ghee to the chart after chanting a sacred mantra for 100008 times.

Guru: Muthu, if we don't get an answer to this question in next 4 hours, we will stop. By the end of 5000th chant, we should have a picture about the reality.

Muthu: This is a difficult situation. By the position of planets, he should have become an IAS officer. How can my father make a mistake like this?

Guru: Muthu, every incident in this world happens for a reason. Kali might have a different plan.

Muthu: Time should tell.

Guru: There are people who come to this world for a sacred objective. They may not know their originality and the nature will drive them. There are dark forces in this world who intend to destroy such people. They work tirelessly to hamper the progress.

Muthu: Do you mean to say, Narayan is one such person?

Guru: May be, don't know. This pooja should go without hindrances.

The Japa starts. Guru is referring several books to enhance the intensity.

Guru: Ramu, please come here.

Ram: Yes guru.

Guru: Have you seen Narayan?

Ram: Yes, I think the person whom I saw at Nanda's house is Narayan.

Guru: Can you draw him on a paper and bring it immediately.

Ram: I don't know drawing guru.

With closed eyes and moving lips, Guru takes few flowers and drops it on the head of Ram.

Guru: Now you go and try.

Ram goes out of the room.

He can hear loud mantras from inside. After sometime Suganthi goes to the room with a pot of water.

Guru: Suganthi, you take bath and come. I am not able to do this without a third person.

Muthu raises his eyebrows. He starts shivering. His guru had spent years in forests for attaining mantra siddhi. He has solved many issues without help from anyone. Today he is asking Suganthi for help. This is not a simple arithmetic. My father has wrongly prepared a chart but there is more to it. We need to find a fix.

After demise of grandfather. Muthu was sent to guru for learning. It was an arduous journey. The clear instruction was to walk 40 kms and reach the gurukul. 40 kms was like 100 kms as there was no road formation. The entire stretch was full of forest land. He could hear noises of wild animals. Halfway, Muthu felt heavy tiredness. He saw a waterfall and took bath. He also drank some water and ate fruits. He felt very sleepy and laid down. Guru saved him from a dense forest.

Guru: You have passed the test. Bad planets tested you for a while.

Guru taught the first mantra to avoid tiredness and hunger and Muthu grew leaps and bounds thereafter.

The state of affairs today is hard to crack. Kali Ma, please give the power…. What is so special about Narayan that even our Mantra Shakthi is not able to assess?

Ram comes inside with the painting of Narayan. He hands it over to Muthu. He has seen Narayan at a young age. Narayan's face has changed a lot. He has a beard now. This is not old Narayan. A secretive glow has come to his face.

Guru completes his rituals. He closes his eyes and sits for 5 minutes. His face looks dejected. He uses one more mantra and opens his eyes. Muthu sees heavy clouds in the eyes of Guru.

Guru: Muthu did you get any hint?

Muthu shakes his head and says no. Guru looks at Suganthi. She also has no clue.

Guru: Bring his drawing.

Guru locks his eyes at the paper. He goes to deep meditation. He is invoking all his old gurus for the remedy. No answer, no answer, no answer Suddenly, a knock at the door is heard.

Guru: The answer has come. Please open the door.

Muthu: Guru, I did not understand.

Guru: There is man waiting outside with the answer for our problems. Nature has sent him. So please take him inside.

Muthu knows the power of his teacher. But who it can be in this midnight? It is raining heavily. The road might be full of water now. There are no buses in this route after 7 PM. Only a car can take you to this place. If a man has come at this time, he may not be an ordinary person.

Muthu: Ram, please open the door.

Guru: No, Ram should not go. There is a reason why I am telling you, Muthu

Guru gives a flower to Muthu and blesses him.

Guru: This is a turning point in your life. You will go way ahead from today. Go and welcome him.

Muthu walks with cold foot. His heart beat is at a 100-meter race now. He reaches near the main door after crossing two rooms. He remembers the words of his guru. This is a turning point of my life.

He hears the knock again. Door is opened slowly. In the dark, he sees the visitor. During his training, Guru had told him that he may experience events that has no explanation. This may be the first one among them. Rain gains its strength. A sudden thunder occupies the background. The sound echoes in the ears of Muthu. In the light of the thunder, Muthu sees the face of the guest. Guru drops a red flower at the feet of Devi…Another thunder follows…

Chapter - 9

London, 1974, A Sunny day.

John and Brenner have become old. They were enjoying their post-retirement life at a private island nearby UK.

John: Any idea, why we have been called by PM. My daughter's wedding is scheduled next week. I was away when she was doing her schooling here. I wanted to be with her throughout this ceremony.

Brenner: The letter did not have any agenda mentioned in it. He just asked us to come and meet. This may be a casual meet. I hope he may assign us important.

John: And you know, he is not going to meet us. It is his PA who will entertain us.

John speaks with a hush tone. The color of his voice changes to black.

Brenner: What? Who gave you this info.

John: Old habits die hard. I take all the information before any meet. This is why I suspect that we will be given a mission soon that may require a travel.

Brenner: My doctor has advised me to undergo a heart surgery soon so that I can live longer.

John: Brenner, we were regarded as the smartest of undercover operators across colonies. Our pockets were filled with highest of salaries, we were gifted an island as a retirement bonus, we get a heavy pension. What does this mean?

Brenner: We are the costliest of slaves.

John: These days, I am not able to sleep. The amount of blood we spiled in India, is chasing me. The cries of mothers, children. We were wrong. Today we are living on their wealth.

Brenner: You may know, I donate a big amount to an organization in India, annually. Still, sleep stands outside my bedroom.

John: Late realization, Brenner. Will Jesus pardon us for our crimes?

Brenner: I think, we should visit India once. I have heard that a holy dip in Ganges and visit to few temples will wash you of your sins.

John: No john, no place in this world can get us acquitted. Out of this remorse, I even attempted for a suicide.

Brenner: What are you talking? Let us visit India, Nepal and Bhutan for 2 months. If possible, we will go to Himalayas also.

John: Let us see if The PM allows us to do this. We are the costliest of slaves. Our time is not ours.

Two men enters the room. They ask John and Brenner to follow them. They enter a room where lunch is arranged.

They occupy the left side of the table. They will have to wait for the most important person of the meeting.

Soon a tall man enters. He is unhappy and frustrated over something. His face looks pale but as soon as he sees the visitors he smiles and greets them. He is the most powerful minister in the cabinet.

Minister: I am so happy to have you here. I have heard a lot about you. I was very young when you were working for the queen. We are really proud that you have earned a lot of money for the crown.

John: It is our privilege of meeting you today.

Brenner: We have read about you in papers. The PM trusts you the most.

Minister: The lord decides…(Laughs).

The minister is in his thirties. He is the son of the richest industrialist in UK. They are Austrians. They migrated to UK few decades back. His father made fortune in steel business and later became famous in Europe. The rating of this minister is just below the PM. The gentleman is poised to become the next PM. He is backed by a most powerful banker and a power broker.PM entrusts all undercover operations to this minister.

Minister: John & Brenner… we are sorry that we had to call you back after your retirement. The situation is so critical and it needs your expertise.

John and Brenner look at each other. At this old age what help can they do?

Minister: Age is just a number. The kind of experience you have in India, has no replacement. You were the pioneers of our India plan. We decided to have a master plan to keep India under slavery. Your brain devised it but after that you retired and came back to UK. The implementation was done by another set of people and that failed.

John: We were closely watching and we understood. We never expected 500 states to become one country.

Minister: That is fine. India should progress financially but the wealth should come to us. It should be our people ruling them. Fortunately, we were able to control their govt, teach them our style, spread our culture and so on.

Brenner: Right. They are our intellectual slaves.

John: They are also on constant fight with Pakistan and China. Nobody visits Kashmir, the heaven on Earth. We should provide funds to them and keep them under our fold. We will get geometric returns from India.

Minister: The problem is that all our agents in India are no more... Their children have not become prominent personalities except one person. So, we need to have a stronger network in India. We are facing a major challenge in Hindu consolidation there. We also have to make them fight with Muslims always.

John: We shot at the bull's eye in Bengal partition.

Minister: That is just not enough. We are planning to create turmoil in India in the next 1-year period. We need experienced hand to guide our young officers. This is a very big game. The budget is huge. We will finance the current govt. If everything goes well, INDIA will always be our colony but the plan has risks. People with cultural and geographical knowledge of India should handle this.

"Dad, I am sure, they are calling you back. You may miss my marriage. You should not go". Emily, daughter of John cried before the meeting.

John: When should we go, Minister?

Minister: The flight is ready with all necessary things. You may leave now. You will get all support from our diplomats there.

John: I will come in a moment.

John dials his daughter. The phone is ringing ….

Chapter - 10

On the way to govt office, Nanda sees a huge crowd at the temple.

Raghu: Nanda, where were you? I called you several times but you were sleeping. Out of excitement, I ran to the temple. Should we believe this?

Nanda: What is the news?

Raghu: You also will be thrilled after hearing it. Any guesses?

Nanda: Are you telling me or not? Don't make me wait.

Raghu: (hesitantly) Nachiar is alive.

Nanda feels that he is in another universe- a place very far from earth. There are no humans in that globe.... Nanda is alone.

Nachiar who died in front of us is back. So, whose body did we cremate on that day? Where was Nachiar all these days? Why did not he come to the village, if he was alive? Will police investigate all these now?

Nanda falls unconscious. Raghu takes him to the banyan tree. A lady brings a jug of water and sprays it on his face. She gives him some water to drink.

Raghu: Nanda, Nachiar will be coming to the temple now. He will clear all our doubts. There is nothing to worry about it. Ashok is there in the police. He will take care of things.

Nanda: Let us go to his house. I want to see him.

Raghu: Please wait. He will be coming here in no time. He wants to do pooja at the temple and later he will meet us.

A car stops at the entrance. Chettiar visits the temple only on rare occasions. Today is a very special day. Chettiar and Nachiar had very good relationship. Both of them being village elders had regular exchanges in panchayat. They also had weekly discussions on village affairs. Chettiar had a plan to get her daughter married to Nachiar's first son, Velu. Unfortunately, Velu passed away in a car accident. Nachiar was training Velu to be a priest and a protector of the village. People say that Nachiar made few mistakes in the daily pooja of a devata and paid price for it. Others believe that Velu was in love with a rich girl and she killed him for unknown reasons. There is also a story that the girl was a ghost. After demise of Velu, appearance of Muthu, who was 10 years old then, changed to that of Velu.

Chettiar occupies the prime seat in the cement structure around the banyan tree. When any important decision is to be taken, Chettiar comes to the temple and sits there. People generally accept the verdict of Chettiar. He is just and rational in his verdicts.

After few minutes, a bullock cart comes. Muthu and an old man get down the cart. That old man may be his guru. A few seconds later, Nachiar alights.

The crowd is awe struck upon seeing him. Nachiar who was killed by foxes is just in front of them. Is it his brother? There is no difference in looks. He has grown a bit older. Hair is still black. He has maintained the same weight. He is healthy and sound. Beard has become bigger. Where was he all these years?

It was he who saved Narayan. Nanda never got a chance to thank him. The assembly has entire village. Let me wait till the crowd disperse.

Nanda sees Parvathy in the temple. She also came to know about it. She was running to the temple. Angai is also with her. Parvathy is happy that she will get to know the future of their son from Nachiar.

Nachiar sits under the banyan tree, beside Chettiar. He closes his eyes and meditates. Chettiar seems to be happy on seeing Nachiar after 23 years. A police officer comes close to Nachiar and checks him.

Chettiar: It Is our good luck that Nachiar has come back after several years. Now the questions remaining in our mind need to be answered. Whose body did we cremate on that day of flood? Where was Nachiar all these years? Why didn't he visit the village during this time? Why has he come now?

SI comes forward and asks Nachiar to get up. He stands up and SI checks the body of Nachiar with the file. He asks Nachiar to remove his shirt. SI verifies various moles in his body.

SI: Without a doubt, this is Nachiar. If needed, we can do some medical tests and confirm.

Chettiar: Not needed. We know our Nachiar, his looks, his sounds, his way of talking. This is him.

The mass clap for Nachiar. They raise some slogans for him.

Chettiar: For young people who does not know Nachiar, I would like to introduce. He is father of Muthu. Nachiar is a famous astrologer in the village. He also knows tantric poojas. Once the entire village faced a serious problem of water scarcity. You may think it was drought. It was not. We faced the issue during rainy season. Village got heavy rains in that year but wells and ponds went dry. Water bodies were not able to hold the water which came from sky. We brought several officers and scientists from govt departments. Nobody was able to solve the problem. I tried a ritual but it could not stop the drain. We went to Nachiar and requested his help. To our astonishment, we found water in Nachiar's well and pond. Nachiar did poojas and gave yantras to all of us. He asked us to deposit these yantras in all wells and ponds. From the very next day, we found our wells full of water. Nachiar did not take a single paisa from any one of us. A Yakshi was drinking all our waters.

Nachiar: It is all god's grace.

Nanda: Nachiar, you are our god. We are excited to know your story. Where were you till now?

Nachiar: I don't know, if you people will believe me. On the day of flood, after helping Parvathy, I went down to do a pooja. It was raining heavily. Through a Sarbeshwara mantra, I made all foxes to vacate the place. So, I was confident that no animal will disturb my peace. I asked my person to cook food for all and not to use brinjal for curries. A new river took birth in Narikunnu due to floods. It was red in color. I saw several human bodies floating on it. I could not control my mind. I knew one pooja which require a dead body. If we do that pooja, our spiritual power will double. You can do this only once in a life time and that too only if you are lucky. You should never kill a person for this or do this on the body of someone whom you know. My guru once told me that, as per my chart, I have the yoga to do this. So, I took one dead body and started the pooja. After few minutes, the corpse sat in front of me. I did not understand, what was going on. Within seconds, the body split into two. One part took the shape of a fox and the other part became an owl. The bird enlarged herself and it became the size of a mountain. The fox also grew. Then the fox, along with me, got on to the owl. The bird flew with both of us.

Pindrop of silence among the crowd.

Nachiar: After some time, I opened my eyes. I was in an ayurvedic hospital in a village. Vaidya told me that I am fine now and can go home. He informed me that I was admitted to this place when he was a student of Ayurveda. I recollected my village and residence but I did not know how to go back to my village. One day, I saw a man who is from this village and he helped me.

Nachiar sees the man standing far away. He is standing at the back and listening. A sweet smile takes birth on his face. There is a bright round of aura behind his head.

Chapter - 11

Muthu: Appa, are we in a dream ?. Me and my guru were trying our level best to crack the problem. Then you arrived.

They are having lunch together. Suganthi is serving them rice and curries. Nachiar liked his daughter-in-law. She is not only beautiful but also has other qualities.

Nachiar: We need to talk the case in detail. Any way I am happy to see your guru.

Guru: I have heard a lot about you from your father-in-law. Happy to see you. One question remains. Whose body did they cremate?

Nachiar: This village has lot of unanswered questions.

After lunch, all of them are sitting in the main room. Nachiar has the habit of chewing tobacco. Suganthi brings the box with tobacco and arecanut.

Nachiar: I am happy to have a daughter like her.

Suganthi smiles and goes inside.

Nachiar: Bring the chart of Narayan.

Ramu brings it from inside.

Nachiar: Ramu, please go to Nanda and ask him to come here by night.

Nachiar to Guru and Muthu: I have a secret to reveal. You should hear it with composure. This is not to be revealed to anyone.

Guru and Muthu become alert. They know that Nachiar is going to tell something very serious. They are more secrets to his exodus from the village than what he told to the public.

Nachiar: Let us go to the pooja room and I will disclose this in front of the deity.

They sit in meditative posture.

Nachiar: On the day of flood, I was sitting in my room and chanting a mantra to stop rain. I failed even after repeating the mantra for lakh times. Suddenly, a deity appeared. I had never seen that murthy in my life. She asked me to take all villagers and go to Narimalai. I expressed my apprehension regarding foxes. She gave me a mantra that would drive them away. She told me that that was a very important day and I should tread cautiously. I had no other option but to listen to her. I took all people on the top of the hill and made tents. Murthy was guiding me in this. After sometime, the deity disappeared. Suddenly I came to know that labor pain started for Parvathy. There was no lady who could manage this. I prayed to the deity and she appeared. She asked me to repeat my mantras for 1 hr. After 1 hour, she told me that Parvathy will deliver a baby girl now.

Muthu: Baby girl! It was a boy, know.

Nachiar: No, Deity gave me a baby boy and asked me to place him near Parvathy. I was also asked to take the baby girl and give to her. I asked her about the boy. Whose boy it was and like. She did not reply. I kept the baby boy near Parvathy and handed over the girl to the murthy. I have never seen that murthy again in my life.

Narrative is getting complicated. Who can answer? How could Nachiar exchange babies in that rain and when people were around?

Nachiar: Narayan is not an ordinary person. He has some great purpose in life. He is unaware.

Muthu: Appa, What about the horoscope? How accurate is it? Nanda anna showed me the chart. On seeing itself, I understood that, it is not Narayan's.

Nachiar: It was prepared by me. On the day of his birth, Nanda asked me to draw the chart. I did not know what to do. In that heavy rain, I called my upasana murthy. He guided me in this. He told me that no one can prepare the chart of this boy.

Muthu: What is secrecy behind his birth and life? What is his Lakshya? Do you have any idea about it?

Nachiar: I tried several times to find it out but failed. I asked my murthy but he did not reveal.

Guru: Sacred births are like this. There will be lot of grey facts behind them.

Nachiar: Muthu, please keep these details away from Nanda. He will not be able to withstand it.

Muthu: Nanda anna's elder sons also faced several life threats during childhood. Is this connected with Narayan?

Nachiar: May be, we don't know. Only time will tell the truth.

Muthu: I request guru to be with us until this game ends.

Guru: I will be with you, don't worry but all these are above our power and knowledge.

Nachiar: These will not be revealed with ordinary poojas. We will have to go to wild forests, if needed.

Muthu: Nanda anna will come by evening. What should we tell?

Guru: Let him come. We will see.

Guru and Nachiar are sitting in the courtyard. Nanda comes along with Parvathy. They are in a happy mood as Nachiar has returned. Nachiar gets up and hugs Nanda.

Nanda: How are you anna? Where were you till now? The village lost its father when you went.

Nachiar: Everything is pre-decided Nanda. We can't do much.

Nanda: We all were very pained. Still, I don't whom we cremated.

Nachiar: Past is past. Let us live in the present. Where is Narayan?

Nanda: He will come in few minutes. He was with us. He met an old friend and is speaking to him.

Nachiar: I wanted to tell you about Narayan. Before that I want to know about his childhood, his academics, his friends and so on.

Nanda: You are a famous astrologer. You may know everything about a person upon seeing him. Why are you asking like this about my son?

Nachiar: HA HA, what you told is right but I need a complete description about him. I will slowly tell you the reason.

Nanda: You know Nachiar that Nanda is my 5th child. We had 3 sons and 1 daughter before Narayan. We had been facing several problems since his birth. On the eighth month of conception, one day, we were working on the field. My elder son came running and told that Parvathy is missing. I ran to my house. A day prior to that, an old lady visited our house. She asked Parvathy to show her left hand. That lady asked my wife to abort the pregnancy as this child would give big trouble to us. Parvathy did not agree. Any way it was 8th month and nothing could be done. That lady told Parvathy that she could do abortion very safely, though it is 8th month. When Parvathy denied it again, that lady cursed her and left our home. Many people advised me to file a missing case with Police but I was sure that Parvathy would return. The village searched her one whole night but we could not find her. Later we saw her in a pool of blood in the forest. Immediately, we took her to the Vaidyar. She was saved after a treatment of 7 days.

Nachiar: I think, I have heard of all these. I know till the birth of the child very well.

Nanda: We had several challenges in his child hood. He was a very bright student till 9th class. Everything went for a toss in that year. He lost focus in studies due to bad company of boys. We could not believe, it was our son. He failed in tenth class. He did some business with a friend in Madurai for 3 years. One fine day, he left the village. We don't know the reason.

Nachiar: He had some altercation with Chettiar, right.

Nanda: Those were minor issues. I spoke with Chettiar on those days, He had no problem.

Nachiar: Where was he all these days? Has he told anything?

Nanda: No. We have no idea regarding that.

Nachiar sees Ram running towards him. He is totally afraid. He wants to say an important thing. He is gasping and he says it at last.

Brahma has stabbed Narayan and he is bleeding profusely. We should take him to hospital immediately.

Nachiar and Nanda runs towards the main road. Parvathy falls down.

Journalist- There is an announcement of landing. 30 minutes left to touch Mumbai. Can I see the climax before that. If the dream is broken, money spent on pass will dissolve in air.

Chapter - 12

Away from Kalikapuram- deep inside a Himalayan Forest.

An old priest is sitting in the middle of a circle of people. The people are chanting some slokas loudly. Guru is listening to these with closed eyes. After an hour the sound stops.

Guru: With this, your Bharata Veda class ends and now you people are free to go back to your villages. You are picked by Trimurthies to save this country. So please do not misuse these mantras.

One Student: Guru, you taught us the entire Bharata Veda but you have not told us why this Veda is not known to general public.

Guru: Suresha, I know you wanted to ask me this question for long. I know this question has been troubling your mind. I was about to tell you people regarding this and this is the time for it.

Suresha: Sorry guru, I was curious about it.

Guru: No Suresha, Curiosity is the basic quality of a student. Tomorrow morning you people can leave to your places. I will tell you before that.

Guru goes back to deep stillness. An old man comes running to guru. He waits for guru to open his eyes.

Guru: Devi knows everything. The world revolves around her wishes.

Old Man: But this is extreme. He has not even started his work there. What will be the end to it?

Guru: He is the best student and greatest of soul. One day Bharath Mata will keep him in her heart. He is poised to achieve great things. He has to bring back the lost glory. So, there will be lot of difficulties. Nature is giving him the training. You don't worry, he will come back.

Old Man: My mind was burning.

Guru: Sanjaya, what is your age now?

Old Man: I don't know, I was born in this place and is living still here. My hair has grown white. My muscles have become weaker but my eyes and ears are working properly.

Guru: We all are here for more than 5000 years. We will be here till this sacred land becomes the strongest one in the world. We will go back once the purpose is met.

Sanjaya cooks food for everyone in the ashram. He does not sleep. He has no idea about his birth. He has never gone outside this ashram. Sanjaya knows only cooking but he has got powers to understand an predict things.

Sanjaya goes back to his kitchen. He has to prepare lunch for the day. Guru does not eat anything. The lunch is for students. Some days, guru asks students not to eat and on those days, he takes rest. Sanjaya once asked guru to train him on the mantra that keeps hunger away. Guru replied that learning mantras is not there in his fate for this Janma.

He will have one more life and in that he will be a great tantric.

The ashram glows but that a prophetic silence. Inhabitants never know about themselves. Only information they have about is that they have come here to learn BHARATH VEDA. They don't know about their birth places, parents or any other details.

Suresha once asked Guru – How will they go back to their places if they don't know the route.

Guru replied- Once you step out of this place, you will automatically remember about you and your place.

Now there are about 300 students here. All of them came on a single day. On the day of last class of previous batch, guru called Sanjaya and instructed him to prepare for next batch. He told that 300 people will come the next day.

There are no ladies in the ashram. Sanjaya asked about this to guru. He was stunned upon hearing the reply. Guru told-Many students living there are girls. Any girl who comes to the ashram will get converted to a boy. After completing the studies, she will get back her original form. Guru will identify girls who are capable of learning BHARATH VEDA through third eye. He will select her when she becomes 17. She may have joined her degree classes in a college. She will be given a privilege to have presence in both ashram and the college at the same time. The girl will learn the Veda at ashram and her degree at college. Nobody will have any doubt as she is available in college every time.

Sanjaya never dared to ask about the guru. Guru always explains about Rama and Krishna as if he has seen them. Sanjaya doubts that this guru was born in Krita yuga. Sanjaya has also seen him dancing thandava in air.

Next day morning the batch of students got up very early. They all are eager to know about the Veda. There are also excited about going back to their original residences.

Guru: Dear Students, I am very glad that you all have completed your course on BHARATA VEDA. Do you have any idea regarding the time you have spent here?

Suresha: No guru. We don't know how many years did we spent here. We feel as if we came here last night. In these days, we never felt hunger. We did not feel sorrow or happiness. We forgot everything and dedicated ourselves to the studies. Morning, evening and night were same for us.

Guru: Good Suresha, I'm happy for your involvement. 6 years have passed after you reached here. When you go back to your homes, many changes would have happened. Pl be wary of it. First thing, you will forget what you have learnt here.

Suresha: What?

Guru: Yes, you will.

Suresha: Guru, then what was the purpose of these years?

Guru: Good question. Though you will generally disremember this, you will be able to recall this when needed. That will be decided by nature.

Sureha: Guru, please tell us in detail.

Guru: Please chant the first sloka of this Veda.

Suresha: Oh, this great bhumi, that was never created and that cannot be destroyed…Oh this great bhumi that is the abode of greatest of souls. Oh, this great bhumi that is the center of the earth and that powers the earth.

Guru: Yes, that is….. Vyasa wrote 5 Veda's. Out of this he kept BHARAT VEDA as secret and disseminated 4 other vedas. Bharat Veda can be learnt only by luckiest of people who are selected by Brahma, Vishnu and Siva. This is the only place where you can learn this. Bharata is the place from where Mother Earth is getting the energy to survive. This Veda was created to protect this country. Our country always face's multiple challenges and it is imperative that few sacred souls learn this to save Bharata from disintegration. We already lost several places like Pakistan but the heart of our country is still intact. This Veda is not written anywhere. I am the only person in this world who can remember this Veda throughout my life. I have been living here since ages. Once you go out of this ashram, you will forget your life here. You will be able to identify problem which our country may encounter. Nature will remind you of these slokas and you will have to use them in need. Now it is your time to leave.

All of them does a Dhanda namaskar and goes out of the ashram. Guru sees them off and goes back to meditation.

Journalist-The plane has landed. Let me continue this dream till air hostess asks me to alight.

Chapter - 13

Nanda and Parvathy are sitting in front of the operation theatre. Sita has come after her school. The entire family and Raghu are a worried lot. How could this happen in day light? Nachiar and Muthu were in hospital till now. They went out to meet Chettiar. Both of them are planning a pooja to save Narayan.

Brahma is the old friend of Narayan. Parvathy has not heard of any kind of dispute between both of them till this day. Brahma has been a regular companion of Narayan to Madurai for businesses. After Narayan left the village, nobody has seen Brahma roaming around in the village. Brahma continued his business in Madurai. Once in a while, when he comes to the village, he pays a visit to Nanda.

People started saying that he has gone mad after Narayan's migration. What could be the reason for the attack? Villagers are asking each other regarding this.

It is the nature of people to create theories when something like this happens in a place. Villagers hatched multiple stories behind the attempt. Some are saying that Narayan left the village with few lakhs of rupees of Brahma. Others have a different version. According to them, Brahma was in love with a girl and Narayan promised him that he will get both of them married.

Believing on his promise, Brahma married that girl in Madurai. On that day, Narayan went missing. Relatives of the girl kidnapped her and roughed up Brahma. The third cook up is that Brahma is in love with Sita and there was an altercation between both of them.

Brahma is absconding. Some boys who were playing cricket saw Brahma boarding a bus to Coimbatore, few hours back. He was not wearing a shirt and was drunk. He was carrying a hen with him. Boys could hear him laugh loudly. He stood in the middle of the mud road to stop the bus. When the bus stopped, he rushed in and threw the hen out. It was a dead hen. Boys ran towards the hen and picked it. They planned to prepare biriyani with it. An old lady advised them to throw it away, take a bath in the pray to Kali till midnight but the boys made fun of it and ran away. Later the police found those boys and questioned them.

Tamil stands muted in front of the theatre. Nobody can console her. She comes to Sita and rests her head on her shoulder. It was just few days back that Narayan agreed for the marriage. She went to her uncle and talked to him after a long time. It is rare to see a politician cry. Uncle wept and later he blessed her. He also told that he will try to get a job for Narayan. Tamil slept peacefully that night. Next morning, she got this news. Brahma is her friend too. He mocks her whenever they meet. He was one among very few who knew about the love affair of Narayan and Tamil.

Nanda sees a group of Policemen coming towards him and there is Ashok in it. A new SI has joined last week. People have already made a positive opinion about him.

SI: You are Narayan's father, right.

Nanda: Yes Sir.

SI: Tell us about the incident. Before that, who are these people.

SI Points towards the family.

Nanda: My wife, daughter, sons and ……

He pauses for a while.

SI: And…. who is she?

Nanda: She is Narayan's friend…. Childhood friend.

Eyes of SI falls at Tamil and comes back to Nanda.

SI: Tell me now, who is this Brahma and why did he try to kill your son?

Nanda: They were good friends sir. Me and my son were going to meet Nachiar and we saw Brahma on the way. Upon seeing Narayan, Brahma hugged him. Narayan and Brahma were taking and I walked to meet Nachiar. After some time, Ram ran to us and….

Nanda broke down…. He sat on the floor. SI tries to pacify him. Parvathy is in tears. There is no bindi on her forehead. Sits has come after an exam in school. Brothers are planning an attack on Brahma but has decided to keep it in abeyance.

SI: Don't worry, Nanda… Our police team at Coimbatore will arrest Brahma there. Ashok will take personal interest in this.

A group of people are sitting under the banyan tree in temple compound. Most of them are chewing pan. Poojari is yet to open the temple. Sun is about to say good bye for the day. It is very exciting to see sun set from the temple premises. Many people can see sun going down and coming back thrice before finally settling down. It is believed that it is specifying three gunas of devi. If you stand outside the place, you will not be able to see this.

Villager: Chettiar is not seen in the village now. Is there a chance that Chettiar has done it through Brahma?

Another: I don't think. Chettiar is not the same person as he was ten years back. The problem between Narayan and Chettiar was settled then only.

Villager: What was the issue between them?

Another: If you ask me, I also don't know. People are quoting different instances. I think it was just a minor one. One day, I saw both of them having heavy debate in front of the temple. People were advising Narayan to calm down. Narayan wanted to marry Tamil but her uncle planned to get her married to Chettiar's son.

Villager: I am going to meet Nanda at hospital. Do you want to come?

Another: Yes, let me also come with you.

They are about to leave the temple. Soon a car comes and stops in front of them. People inside the car throws a big sack to the compound. There is someone inside the packet. Both of them run towards it.

Villager: Should we open it or call the Poojary?

Another: I think, it is better to call him and consult. Also ask Raghu and others to come.

Next moment, the sack was in the middle of the crowd. Poojary notices a lemon lying with the pack. He prays to Kali Ma.

Raghu opens it with a knife. Everybody comes closer to it.

A shock passes through the body of Raghu and he sees Brahma inside the cover along with a hen.

Chapter - 14

A big sound of OHM resonates inside Narayan. He wakes up with a new light on his face. He sees himself inside an operation theatre. Doctors are around him and nurses are busy in preparing medicines. Suddenly he sees THE GURU sitting in front of him. He is in Padmasana.

Narayan sees a big ball of energy getting inside his body.

Doctors have completed their work. The team is preparing to leave the theatre.

Doctor: Miracle…what else could I say about this? Do you know, he was brought dead. Our nurse was going to shift the body to mortuary. His heart started beating after that. We immediately planned a surgery and we are done.

Nurse: I have never seen such a recovery in my career. He will be Ok in 1 week.

Doctor: Take care of him till he becomes conscious.

Doctors and junior nurses move out to their rooms. Now only head nurse is seen. She is checking the medicine box.

Narayan is able to see the room in his sub conscious mind. The place is completely immersed in the light of Himalayan Guru.

Guru: Narayan, please chant the Raksha mantra of Bharat Veda.

Narayan: Oh, the universe, I was in dark. Then a strong gush of water came towards me…I had no option but to create a check dam…The water was so strong that finally it washed away both me and the construction…The flood took me to an unknown island. Now I am playing the dual role of King and the beggar in the island…Soon I will see a rescue ship and the boat will take me to that ship.

Narayan is in tears after chanting this for the first time. Guru asks him to do mantra Japa for 108 times. After completion, Narayan opens his eyes.

Narayan: Guru, what is the objective of my life? Who am I? Why is this happening to me?

Guru: Son, all these questions will be answered by nature as you grow. You are just 23 now. You have a great purpose of life. As God has sent everyone with an objective, yours is a special one.

Narayan: What was the secret of teaching me the fifth Veda? I don't even remember a single verse. Only after seeing you I could recall the Raksha mantra.

Guru: Do you recollect the day when you left our Ashrama? I called you personally and explained all these?

Narayan: I can't bear this anymore guru. I am a pain for everyone including my mother. I even thought of suicide.

Narayan goes to a deep sleep. He sees a beautiful dream. His past comes and stands in front of him. Yes, he is in 8th standard. Uma teacher is conducting Math classes. She appreciates Narayan for his numerical skills. It is time for the closure of the session. She leaves the class. Tamil comes and takes his notes and goes through it.

Tamil: You have scored 100 out of 100 for Math, 90 for science… Math teacher calls you Ramanujan and Science teacher wants you to become C V Raman. What will you become, Narayan?

Narayan: I want to become both. (Laughs)

One day Narayan hears math teacher telling head master that school should provide special care to Narayan. He may become very popular in the field.

In another scene, he sees his parents, stitching a wish, that is as big as the globe. They wanted him to become district collector and help a lot of people in the village. Parvathi wants him to help farmers to find a stable income. Demand of Nanda is a safe and secure home for the poor.

His mother had seen women cooking in blue flame in cities. She wants Narayan to help the village women to get that. She also thinks of her son helping the village to get rid of drinking water problem.

Narayan is in Independence Day celebrations now. He has heard of freedom struggle. The village has a small library promoted by a freedom fighter. Most of the books are related to Mahatma, Subash Chandra Bose. Patel, Nehru and people like Bhagath Singh and Asad. Narayan has almost finished reading them. The freedom fighter has promised him to get new books from other places. Narayan spends his time with the freedom fighter on weekends. The gentleman has advised him to read newspapers and create opinion on current affairs. He sees a great politician in Narayan who can contribute to the nation.

Head Master is ready to hoist the national flag. The school band is playing the anthem. A shiver passes through Narayan as the flag moves upward. He sees a blue light beside the flag and it gains size as it reaches the zenith. He could not see anything. Clouds cover the landscape of his eyes and soon it starts to rain. One sentence in the speech of head master beats in his heart till now. Fall down on Bharatha Matha and you still can smell the blood, the sweat, the tears and dreams dropped by millions of our countrymen. She has embraced them close to her chest and they will always live in HER.

Why did Narayan cry during flag hoisting? Tamil asked him. He did not reply. He asked a counter question to her. Did you see any blue light along with the flag. She said no. Not only her. No one else saw that. He was the only person who could see that light.

The next day, Brahma sees Narayan sitting alone and thinking something.

Brahma: Dey, nowadays you are always alone. Why can't you come and play with us? We are missing you a lot. I know you are always behind Tamil. Spend some time with us also da.

Narayan: Brahma, nowadays I don't know what is happening to me. I feel very tired. I don't get interest in studies. I think I should go to some other place. I have not been going to temple also these days.

Brahma: Don't worry, I have medicine for this.

Narayan: Really. I would like to see that.

Narayan and Brahma are travelling on a bicycle. Soon they see forests on both sides. Deep sound of rabbits, peacocks and foxes fills the background. Some trees are touching the road through branches. The place is also full with dens. Brahma is very familiar with the location. Brahma is narrating the story of this place. This was a sprawling town 300 years ago. The town was ruled by a powerful king who had 8 wives. He was like a slave to the most beautiful wife. One day, both of them were travelling to their winter palace and they saw a swami with his wife who was more beautiful than King's wife. Queen considered herself as the most beautiful women in the town. The jealousy in her planned to exterminate swami's wife and regain her first position. She made King to invite Swami to be the Rajpurohit. Swami was a very poor man and he became happy on this. Both of them shifted to the palace on same day. Queen befriended swami's wife and finally poisoned her. She told Swami that a snake killed her . Upon hearing this sad news swami left the palace to Himalayas to do tapas. Queen was happy that she again became number one. That was the beginning of the decline. As the penance of swami progressed, the town started losing its glory and soon became a forest. Several diseases attacked the queen and she died. It is believed that ladies are not allowed in the forest. Spirit of queen is wandering in the place. She will harm any girl who is beautiful.

Brahma stops the cycle. From here they have to walk another 2 kms to reach the site. It was evening when they left their village. Now it is late evening. Narayan is afraid.

He has not told his mother about this. Today being Amavasi, she may think that he is in temple. So, he is safe.

A big hill appears. Now a steep climb.... He is already tired of cycle journey. This will take 1 hr.

Brahma: Your worries are going to end, brother. We will reach in 10 minutes.

Narayan sees the blue light passing above his head. The same light which he saw on Independence Day. It is waiving at him. They are in front of a water fall. This is bigger than Nayagra. Is it a dream? If it is not a dream, then why are we taught that Nayagra is the biggest waterfall?

Monkeys are running around. Brahma takes one banana and throws at them. A smart one catches it and climbs a tree. Smarter ones are running towards him for more bananas but he had only one.

Hey wait...a big shout and monkeys go back to trees. who is it, such a strong sound. A tall man with long hair...a man with fiery eyes splits the darkness and comes out.
How are you Brahma and Narayan? The sound asks.

Now they can see him clearly. Brahma smiles at him and falls at his feet.

Narayan lives in surprise. People say that there are 7 people with similar cant this be true? Is it the same person or am I seeing his dupe?

Chapter - 15

Chettiar…Chettiar is the person in front of us. But he is taller than Chettiar. He is black and this person is fair. This is not him. Narayan concluded.

Person: How are you, Narayan? I am not your Chettiar. I am Ananthan. friend of your father. Go and ask your father about me.

Narayan: I have heard of you. Father has told me. I never thought that you look like Chettiar.

Ananthan: You can stay here tonight. We will have lot of fun

Ananthan asks both of them to take bath and come for dinner. The cool water flows through their bodies. The dinner is ready with nuts, fruits and non veg.

A very beautiful girl is serving them the food. Her hair is very long and touches the ground. Narayan is in a new world.

After the dinner, Ananthan calls both of them. Now there is a smoke around Ananthan.

Ananthan: Brahma told me about your problems. All your frustrations will go away in single medicine. Take this before you sleep today. I will give you 100 golies tomorrow before you go.

The girl gives him water to take the tablet. Immediately after having it, he flies to the sky. He sees the full moon there. Today is new moon day. How can you see the full moon? Stars are talking to each other. They are really playing cards. Moon is giving them white wine and after drinking it they run around. Narayan is sitting on a star and it takes him around the universe. On the other part, he sees sun. It is too hot. So, he asks the star to take him back to moon. He lands at moon and there is a big hill of mangoes in it. He gets on to it and eats few mangoes. Soon the hills turn into a forest of grapes. Narayan makes wine out of them.

Next day morning, Ananthan shares a pack with Narayan.

Ananthan: Take it for free, you are son of my Nanda. Go ahead and live life.

They reach the village by 12 PM next day. By that time, it was a big news in the locality. Both of them are missing. Narayan has entered an unfamiliar place. He is very tired. He lays down and sleeps. In the sleep, Stars again come and offers a ride on them.

Narayan is still in the hospital bed. The dream continues……

Now he is a school drop out. Tamil has passed the exam and scored good marks. She is planning to join intermediate course. Narayan does not know the way out. Every week he goes to Ananthan to collect medicines. Brahma and Bairava became close friends. Their main business is selling medicines at Madurai. They have taken a house on rent there... Even when they come to village, they sit at temple. Business is very profitable and Bairava has purchased a car. Their next aim is to produce a film.

Nanda, Parvathi and the head master are concerned about the way things had shaped up. They expected the child to become a super hero and he turned to be a villain. Nanda has started giving up. He only knows that they are doing some illegal business. One day, he saw Ananthan in Bairava's car but Parvathi has not believed all these stories. She is sure that her son won't do bad business.

The car is moving at heavy speed. Bairava is inebriated and is singing songs. It is very difficult to see the road in thick darkness. Brahma is changing songs frequently. They are going to the village for festival. Narayan looked at the sky through the window pane. Sky also seems to be in an delighted mood. Suddenly the blue light appears. This light has been with him since the Independence Day celebrations at school. He does not understand why the light comes and goes. One day he asked an astrologer regarding this. He replied that it may be an illusion but Narayan has not believed it. There is more to this light than it appears. The light is moving with the car.

In another 30 minutes, they will reach the temple for the yearly festival. By the way, Bairava drives, they may even reach much before that.

Temple looks like a palace with all colors blended on it. Narayan remembers his old days when they were kids. His only attraction during the festival was Tamil and break dancers. Tamil looked more beautiful on such occasions.

The Fifth Veda

A big stage is set in the compound. They will be a display of a movie after 10 PM. Every festival season a major demand of people is exhibition of a movie. Guna has gone to get the tapes from a nearby city.

Narayan and team are in queue for food. A tall man approaches them. He looks at Narayan and Brahma. His eyes slide to Bairava.

Tall man: Why are you late? People are agitated. Give the pack.

Bairava takes a big pack from his bag and hands it over to the man. The man again looks at Brahma and Narayan before going back.

Bairava to tall man: Don't worry. They are my people.

The man walks away without looking back.

Brahma: Bairava, we have a decent medicine business and why should you do this dirty one?

Bairava: Brahma, you just came from Madurai to this village on the car brought by that dirty business. So, keep quiet.

Narayan: Stop this, Bairava.

Bairava: Who are you people to advise me? I brought you to this business and now you have all the money. Do you think that medicine business is righteous?

Narayan: What is wrong? We are supplying medicines at cheap rate and people are benefitting from it. In your case, people are ruined.

Bairava: Now I am not for a fight. I want a peg. Are you coming?

Narayan: No, today you will have to answer my questions.

Brahma: Narayan, forget it. We will discuss tomorrow and let us enjoy the party for the moment.

Narayan: No, I think we are doing something wrong.

Bairava: Yes, we are doing wrong but let us do another wrong thing now. Come for the drink.

The gang walks towards the ground near to the temple pond. They see a big crowd making ludicrous sounds after boozing. The team joins them.

Narayan sees that blue light again. The light comes down from the sky and flies towards him. It reaches the ground and makes a circle around him and goes back to the sky. Before leaving, it says in his ears- "Get ready for a travel".

A man with white shirt and dhoti appears. A well-built, good looking man with thin mustache. He greets Narayan. He requests few minutes of him.

The man: Narayan, do you remember me? I am Sekar. I am your senior in school. We shifted to Bangalore after my 5 STD.

Narayan: Oh, Sekar… after how many years? It is a surprise. I would have eaten at least 1000 mangoes from your yard. What are you doing now?

Sekar: I will tell you in detail but I want you to come with me to my house.

Narayan: I will come tomorrow. Today my friends won't leave me.

Sekar: No man, this minute you have to come with me. It is a serious matter.

Narayan could smell the gravity. Sekar is visiting the village after several years. He had been a nice guy to Narayan. Very good in English and general knowledge. Identifying his talent, Sekar was sent to Bangalore by his father for better environment. . .

Narayan and Sekar flies away leaving behind a set of unruly guys with alcohol running in their veins. Is the vehicle running at more than 150 km per hour? Narayan is moving ahead of time and for forever.

Chapter - 16

It is a small and traditional house with a mini forest and a playground. Sekar's father owned 1000 acres. He was part of the axis-Nachiar, Chettiar and Sekar's father. Any decision taken by them went unopposed. Nachiar provided the spiritual power, Chettiar the muscle power and the third one, the money power. They ruled the village for many years. There are multiple stories weaved for the exit of Sekar's family from the village. They sold the land bank to Chettiar except the house and adjunct land. On the day of travel. thousands of people gathered at the house. They did not cry but requested Sekar and family to visit the village once in a year. Father passed away last year. Sekar is living with mother and wife.

Journalist-Can I make one statement about this? - It is customary for shameless guys to eat wealth of gullible.

Sekar: How are you, Narayan? What are you doing?

Brotherly love is evident in his voice. Sekar looked at his eyes He sees a completely changed Narayan.

Narayan: We are doing small scale business of medicines.

Sekar: We mean? Who all?

Narayan: Me, Bairava and Brahma.

Sekar: Friend, let me tell you the fact. Do you know that I am working as an IPS officer?

Narayan: Great, I am not aware of it. Congratulations....

Sekar: My father predicted this when I was 5. He also believed that one of my close friends will become an IAS officer. Do you know who it is?

Narayan:?

Sekar: It is you.

Narayan's eyes go down for 2 minutes.... They look at each other...Sekar with pain and Narayan with regret.

Sekar: You are just 17.... You still have time...I am 8 years elder to you. Please take my advice. Write your exams, do your graduation and go for it. Loosing 3 years does not matter.

Narayan: Anna, I don't know what happened to me. I am in control of others.

Dam opens in his eyes. The water moves towards the catchment area. Sekar is also in tears.

Sekar: I want you to come with me to Bangalore. You can join the classes there.

Narayan is in contemplation....... Leaving Brahma and Bairava is a difficult task but Sekar is right. I have to get back to studies.

Sekar: You tell me. I met your father today and explained him all these.

Sekar gets a cup of coffee and snacks. Narayan holds the cup and sips through.

Sekar: I have an important matter to discuss. What do you sell? From where do you get this?

Narayan: We trade medicines. These are cheaper.

Sekar: From where do you buy this?

Narayan: That I don't know. It is from Madurai. I know only that much.

Sekar: Company name?

Narayan: I don't know.

Sekar: Who does the purchase?

Narayan: Bairava.

Sekar: Only he? Brahma is not involved, right?

Narayan gets embarrassed. He can sense danger. You are taking to a Police Officer.

Sekar: Narayan, you are in a big trap. I can save you from this, only if you cooperate with me.

Narayan: I will tell whatever I know.

Sekar: I was called by Chief Minister of Karnataka a few days ago. He assigned me a job. There is a racket doing the business of ganja in Tamil Nadu and they are the main suppliers of the contraband in Karnataka. The mafia is based out of Madurai. Do you know the leader's name?

Sekar takes a photo from his pocket and shows it to him. Narayan looks at that and sits in shock. Narayan wipes his eyes and checks again. This is Bairava...

Sekar: So, get out of this immediately. In next few days, they will be behind bars. We have evidence. I have collected few documents. I want you to be out of this. Your name is also there in the list but I will manage it.

Narayan: I had suspicion…I have seen Bairava handing over packets to unknown people.

Sekar: Then why did you continue their company?

Narayan: I have no option.

Sekar: It is your decision.

Narayan: Please save Brahma. He is not aware of it.

Sekar: I can't promise that. From now, you should not even talk to those people.

Narayan: I have Rs 1 Lacs of Brahma. What should I do?

Sekar: Hand it over to me for the time being. I will see what to do. Please go and sleep at your house for the moment. We will talk tomorrow. Keep all secrets with you. Come, I will drop you.

Narayan: No….

Narayan is walking on the street alone. The night is very dark. There are no street lights around. Narayan wishes if he gets a torch. On the left side of the road, he can see temple glowing in happiness. Bairava and Brahma might be having their bash. He can't even think of Bairava getting into such businesses. Today, Narayan is the friend of a mafia king.

Narayan decides to go to Bangalore. He wants to attain the position which he dreamt of. Nanda and Parvathy had seen a lot of colors around him. It will be a support to them, if he earns and feeds the family. Seetha will be old enough to get married in another 10 years. Someone has to take care of her needs. Money is the key and it is to be acquired through genuine methods. Narayan decides to go back to Sekar and confirm his offer. He has to stroll back few miles to see Sekar but this will be the turning point of his life.

Gates in front of his house is open. Narayan had closed it before going. Who else would have opened it? There is no light inside the house. Sekar might have slept. It may be inappropriate to wake him up at this time. Naryan thinks about his old friend. How good is this guy? Else why would someone like him save Narayan from disgrace.

Suddenly, he hears a big laughter from the house. There are people more than 2. One of them is Sekar. Noone was there when Narayan met Sekar. Now, who has come? Queries after queries covered his mind. He can hear people speaking in between.

"I told you he is a trickster. You asked me to include him in the team"

"I never thought, he is a crook…what should we do now?"

God, this is Bairava. He is speaking to Sekar. What is happening here?

"CM has sent me here to arrest the mafia king. Narayan, the mafia king."

Narayan is shocked to hear this. Is it the same Sekar who was taking to him, an hour ago. What is his connection with Bairava?

"What about Brahma?"

"He will go back to Brahma loka…"

Are they serious? How can a close friend like Brahma be killed. Are they human?

What should I do now? Oh, Ma Kali, show me a way. Can I go and tell Brahma regarding this? He is a soft person. He will not be able to crack this. God, where have I reached? A death knell…. How will I move out of it. Two lives are hanging in balance- Brahma and Narayan. Can I discuss with Chettiar or Ananthan? No, it has become difficult to believe anyone. The person who seemed to be a messiah, has now become a demon. The road ahead is bumpy.

Narayan sits on the road with his hands on the chest. He feels a pain in his spirit. There is only one power to help him……. only one power….

Journalist- Yaar…It is my turn to get down. The dream is over. It was worth watching the movie. What will happen to our champion? How will he escape from this Chakravyuh? Was this the exact reason for his evaporation? How will he save himself? My mind wanders in lurch.

My phone rings- "AP Sir?"

Other Voice- "I am your cab driver. I am waiting outside the airport"- A divine vibration is evident in those words. The whole negative energy built up fades away. I picked my baggage and walked away.

Chapter - 17

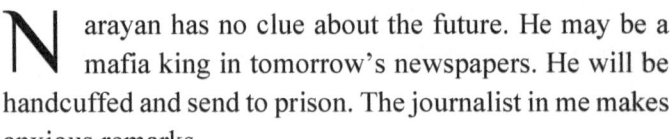

Narayan has no clue about the future. He may be a mafia king in tomorrow's newspapers. He will be handcuffed and send to prison. The journalist in me makes anxious remarks.

The cab driver seems to be a divine person. He is speaking in Gujarati over phone. I like all Indian languages and can follow some.

Cab Driver: Sir you are worried about something?

AP: How could you guess this?

Cab Driver: I can read faces and at times mind.

AP: Are you an astrologer or a mentalist?

Cab Driver: I am an AAM ADMI…but I know you are searching for answers.

AP: Chalo, tell me what is in my mind?

Cab Driver: You were seeing a dream and you woke up in between.

What? This man can see my mind. I had no words.

Cab Driver: I can complete the story sir. I will tell you what happened to Narayan after that night.

Am I in a supernatural world? This person has got some powers.

Cab Driver: Today morning, I got two ride options- One with you and another to Jaipur. My mind asked me to select yours. My inner voice told me that there is a purpose behind it.

AP: How do you know Narayan?

Cab Driver: I don't know him. You saw the first part of the dream and I saw the second part. My soul told me that some day, I will have to narrate the dream to a good person who has seen the first part.

The world is perplexing…. Lips of the driver will take us back to 1974.

The night is long in front of Narayan. What will happen if I am not there in this world? If I die, my family will be saved from disgrace. The problems of Sekar and Bairava will end. My short life is going to burst. What all dreams did my parents have? Tamil will marry her cousin and live happily. So, this is the optimum solution. Narayan walks towards the pond. The water will be my final abode. She will embrace me. There is no better place to perform this climax.

Narayan stands beside the pond. The night is very cool. The crowd has left the place. The sound has stopped. Tinkle of my life will also stop soon. This is the pond, where we, as children, learnt swimming. This is the pond, to which we shared many stories. This is the pond, that speaks to us. Pond, save me. Narayan jumps into it. Water of the pond is turning into tears.

God forgive me…I am throwing your precious gift…the life…I have been on the brim…. The fall is inevitable.

Narayan finds himself at the bed of the pond. He is sitting in padmasan.

Yes, he can breathe. What is this? —A miracle or a reverie. He is flanked by water plants. He is sitting on a rock. With closed eyes, Narayan prays to Ma Kali.

A light emanates from the forehead and that turns into the blue light. A strong sound of conch shell reverberates… The blue light turns into a fire and takes a round of Narayan and then settles in front of him.

Blue Light: Narayan, open your eyes.

Narayan: Where am I. What is this magic? I can breathe in water.

Blue light: Son, how are you feeling now?

Narayan: I am in trouble…They will trap me…. the conmen.

Blue Light: Noone can do anything to you. Trust me. This is the time for your enlightenment.

Narayan: Who are you?

Blue Light: I am you, the self in you… I am Jeevathma and I am also the Paramathma.

Narayan: Tell me, how will you save me from this?

Blue Light: Do you understand that you are born to protect this country? Do you realize that you are Suputhra of Bharath Matha?

Narayan: If so, why I have been subjected to bad experiences?

Blue Light: The nature wants to shape you up. Now you have seen both bad and good sides of life. Yours will be a life dedicated to this land.

Narayan: Who will take care of my family?

Blue Light: The nature…nature will.

Narayan: Tomorrow I will be regarded as a criminal. I will be apprehended by police.

Blue light: That will not happen. You will leave this village tonight. I will guide you…You will have to come with me.

Narayan: If I leave this village, they will mark me as an absconder and charge all cases against me.

Blue Light: No, do you know that Police Department is aware of the criminals. They have already arrested Sekar and Bairava. Now you can sit peacefully. CM had doubt on Sekar. So, another set of Police was sent to keep him in check.

Narayan: When did this happen?

Blue Light: 2 days back. You and Brahma are not in the list of offenders

Narayan: 2 days back? I have just spoken to Sekar and jumped into this pond.

Blue light: Now you are on a different time zone. You have already spent 5 days in this pond. You were searching yourself.

Narayan could not believe that. What all secrets are revolving around this?

Blue Light: Now get ready…It is time to leave.

Narayan: Tell me. where are we going?

Blue Light: From now, you have no right to ask questions. Just follow my instructions. You should not go to your home. Whatever is needed for you will be provided by the nature. Now you are in the hands of mother nature.

Narayan: One wish…

Blue Light: I know, you can write a letter to Tamil and leave it at her home. You have to come back soon. I will be waiting for you at the Temple

Narayan is now walking on the mud road toward her house. He has to cross Narimalai on the way. It has been 5 days after his last dinner. He did not feel hunger and thirst inside the pond. Now he is tired and weak. Blue light is asking him to get ready for a long journey. Where is the destination?

Narayan felt very bad that he is going to leave this place. How long will it take for the return? When can I meet my family?

My mother…father. Brothers…sisters. I am leaving them for some time. This is for the good of all. I am saved from the ignominy of being a criminal. A candle light is burning in the room of Parvathy…She has not slept.

A loud voice from Nanda says- "Parvathy, you sleep, I will go to police and file a missing compliant tomorrow.

That is about Narayan, they are nervous about his disappearance.

He walks ahead. Another 1 km…

Tamil might be awake. If needed, he can call her through the window. But light has clearly instructed not to meet anyone.

The letter to Tamil Says…

Dear Tamil,

This is the first letter by me. We saw dreams after dreams about life…Life is a magician. He shows something and the reality is something else. I have seen you clapping for magicians' tricks…Life is a cinema…The script is pre decided…The actor has only one option – to dance according to the wishes of the writer. Life has not been benevolent to me. Neither it has been so cruel.

I am embarking on an uncertain journey. The path which may not end. I am following a clock which has figures more than 12.

You are a girl who can float on the river. I am sinking in a stream which has no depth. So, I mean to say that we should part ways…I may or may not meet you again. You will always be in my mind.

Yours

Narayan.

It is 2 AM….. Blue light is very much visible on the peepal tree. Seeing Narayan, it comes down and signals him to follow.

He prostrates before Ma Kali… A voice from the temple says- Go ahead son, I am always with you.

The light starts its journey and the man – the future of Bharath follows. Here starts a historic journey that may end only with Bharat becoming the Viswaguru.

Chapter - 18

Narayan opens his eyes… The operation theatre is full of lights now. Guru is sitting in padmasana. The thickness of air has reduced.

Guru: So, now you understood what exactly happened to you, right?

Narayan: Yes, guru…my mind is able to read the past. When I came back to my home, it was as if I woke up from a sleep. I knew that nature had trained me on powers but I did not know full facts.

Guru: It is your turn. You tell me about your journey from the village till our ashram and what happened in the ashram.

Narayan says…

It was almost 3 days after I left the village. The blue light was moving ahead of me very fast. I had never walked like that in my life. I did not feel like eating or drinking. Light was giving me abundant force to cover the distance.

When people stopped speaking Tamil, I understood that we are out of TN. I started hearing unfamiliar languages. But I could follow all these as blue lights continued to give me powers. I walked all day and night. Finally, we arrived at Kashi. Blue Light told me that there will be a halt of 5 days here. I did not have money to buy food or clothes.

Blue light navigated me to an ashram near ganga. It was a very old building. Night was slowly starting its work. Soon the blue light went off. I was afraid. I did not know the next step. Was I under a hallucination? I called the blue light but to no avail. I sat on the ground.

A swami came out of the building. He asked me if I am Narayan. I could not believe it. He told me that they had been waiting for me. He asked if the journey was fine. I told him that a blue light showed me the way and it is not seen anywhere now. I could not believe that I was speaking in Sanskrit. Swami informed me that I will be able to see the light only after 5 days.

He gave a towel to take bath in ganga. After the bath, we had fruits and vegetables for dinner. He asked me to wake up at 3 AM the next day. I got up at 2 30 AM, took bath and waited for him.

He came in a white dress. He smiled and asked me to sit on the ground.

Swami: How are you feeling Narayan?

Narayan: I don't now swami, I am tired. I don't know my destination. Blue light told me about several great tasks which I have to do but not sure of it.

Swami: You are on your way to Himalayas, my boy. You will be taught several subjects by a Maha guru there. But even I am not sure of those. I know only one thing; you are one among several people chosen to save this country from destruction.

Narayan: I did not understand swami.

Swami: This is a great land gifted by gods to us. This is created by brahma from dust of devi's feet. This is the place that make earth rotate and revolve. This is the sacred land that gives energy to sun and the universe. This is land of devas.

Narayan: You are mentioning about India, our country.

Swami: Yes, the Bharath that extends from Kazhakisthan to Cambodia. The Akhand Bharath which was the golden bird of ancient times.

Narayan: I was not aware of that…Such a big land.

Swami: Yes, as it is a big land of devas. asuras from time to time have been snatching our land. They want to control our country so that the entire universe comes under them.

Narayan: That means who ever rules us will dominate the universe.

Swami: Yes, my boy. I will not be able to tell you the whole story. It is the right of maha guru to brief you on this.

Narayan: Please tell me more swami. I can't hold the excitement.

Swami: Good that you are curious to hear about this. I am sure that you have a great assignment on the way. My duty is different. I have to teach you Sandhya Vandana and 4 Vedas in 5 days. I have to prepare you to go to Himalayas. I have to do your upanayana.

Narayan: That much in 5 days. Is it possible swami?

Swami: This is initiated by gods. They will take care of it.

Swami conducted my upanayana. He asked me to chat gayatri mantra for 1 Lakh times. After the meditation, he asked me to show my right hand.

He held the pointing finger and we sat for hours in that position. I don't know how time passed. I felt that, time machine is taking me to old centuries. We were sitting in a dense forest and swami was teaching me Vedas.

Swami: Open your eyes.

I opened to a new world.

Swami: Chant all 4 Vedas in succession.

Vedas were dancing in my tongue. I saw Saraswati devi sitting beside me and holding my hands. Ganga took rebirth in my eyes. I fell at swami's feet.

Swami: I have one last task. I have to prepare you for your stay at Himalayas. You will forget your past life. Your village and your family will be erased from your mind. Even this Vedas and whatever you learn at the Himalayas will come to your brain only when the country is in trouble. You will have no idea about your super natural powers and will be able to use only when you or the land faces any problem.

He took me to a ground. We both sat on the grass.

Swami: You should have extraordinary will and physical ability to tide over the adversities in Himalayas. The temperature will be very less and the altitude makes oxygen a scarce commodity. It is imperative that you learn yoga sastra to withstand this.

The Fifth Veda

Swami taught me several yoga postures for daily life. He trained me to do Surya namaskar for 108 times. He taught me mantras to control blood pressure and Pranayama to have good breath.

Swami: One thing you should try to get it from the Maha Guru.

Narayan: What is it, Swami?

Swami: Only the luckiest of people gets this. I have spent more than 1000 years in his ashram but he did not teach me that vidya.

Shocked…1000 years…The swami with me is more than 1000 years of age… are these jokes of nature?

Seeing my face, swami asked- Don't worry, The Maha Guru is 5000 years old. Another shock……

Swami: I have seen this land getting assaulted by goons. I have seen loot, cries, desperation, persecution, famine, massacres…I ran to Maha Guru for a solution. Do you know what he predicted?

Narayan: Tell me Swami.

Swami: Someone with energy of 1000 suns will emerge and he will bring this land to glory and he will rule the world. Ok… Forget it. Let me tell you. I am sure you will get it.

Narayan: What swami?

Swami: Maha Guru taught me everything except the Bhumi Mantra. It is the mantra of devi. The most sacred mantra. Only 3 people in this world know it. I want you to be the fourth one. Maha Guru will give it only to the person who has the power to protect the universe.

Narayan: Am I eligible to receive it?

Swami: My mind tells… You are …

Swami kept his hand on my head and blessed me. I was up for a long and arduous journey. I have not even completed 25 % of the trip. Swami asked me to visit all temples in the area and pray. He asked me to sleep peacefully that night. I should get up much early tomorrow to start the journey. I asked him about the blue light. He told me that the light rests in me and will take me to the last stop.

Next day morning, swami did Ganapathy Havan. There were more participants in it. I felt bad that I am leaving the location but everything was for good. The inhabitants of the ashram were in tears. I have been very close to them during the short stint.

There were no emotions on the face of swami. He was smiling. I touched his feet.

Soon my companion, the blue light appeared and sat on my shoulder.

Chapter - 19

Narayan continues…. My legs were paining after the long walk. I immediately applied relief techniques taught by swami. I wondered about the art and science of Indian culture. Swami once told- Indian system of life has several species of knowledge and most of them are endangered ones. If a guru attains samadhi without passing on the mantra to his shishya, the skill may go down the oblivion.

I wanted to acquire maximum wealth and transmit it to the coming generations. I may not be Sankara or Vivekananda but I have to do my part. How did the Maha Guru select me for this role? That remained a question in me. Who am I? What is so special in me?

We started our journey by praying to ganga. Me and blue light took a holy dip. There was Sahasra Ganapati Pooja in ashram. I had a sense of difficulty waiting for me at the travel.

Blue light started moving at a great speed. I found it difficult to cope up. Miles and miles were behind us. The light stopped at a particular place.

Blue light: This place is called Hima Kund. This is a holy pond. Two things should be done before ascending Himalaya. One you have to take a dip in this Kund- Two, you have to pray to Lord Shiva. Those who don't do this before the climb will surely fail.

I saw big Himadri standing on our way. I prayed to Ma Kali to give me power to touch the zenith. This is not just a hill but the center of energy, the abode of lord Shiva. How many more wizardries are waiting for us? The heart in me started making OHM sound.

The temperature within the Kund was very low. A person without mantras will surely freeze. I repeated the Sharath rythu mantra to overcome minus 100 degrees Celsius. An ice berg in the shape of lord shiva is placed in the middle of the Kund. We have to touch the feet and take permission to enter Himalayas. . Har Har Mahadev…. I felt a beam of energy when I touched it.

I decided to meditate in the Kund itself. Blue Light was not expecting that. The light advised me not to spend more time within the Kund. I replied that I will be happy, if I die in this Kund. For each successive invocation of mantras, a new man was taking birth in me.

Blue Light was totally impressed after I completed 6 hours of stay in the Kund. Light was sure that we will comfortably cross the mountain.

We both did Dhanda Namaskar to the hill and started. After few minutes we were welcomed by an icy wind. The storm was creating a dew village around us. Light asked me to stand still for the time being till the air settles. That was another opportunity to invoke Shiva in me. He is the guru of gurus- ADI GURU. I realized that we are passing the way which Shankaracharya walked. I have to keep my mind still on any kind of adversity. Positive images and thoughts should cover my mind. Even a second of wrong thinking would reduce my powers.

We sat to take rest. I saw something big coming towards us. Due to fog, diminished visibility was becoming a barrier. That was moving both sideways and upwards. It is an animal…. It is not a small one. I checked for Blue Light. Swami did not teach me how to handle animals. Mantras were to firewall weather conditions. Can this be the end of my expedition? Can Hima Kund fail? No, how could Lord Shiva not protect me. I closed my eyes. The animal came near to me. I can sense its breath. The face touched my feet, my hands and my face. I did not open my eyes. I understood that the animal has horns. Suddenly I heard Blue Light speaking.

Blue Light: Narayan, open your eyes and see who it is?

My eyes invited me to an unbelievable scene. A big bull, as big as an elephant and it was smiling. Amazing, it started speaking.

Bull: I have come from ashram. Maha Guru sent me to take you to our place. Come, sit on my back and we will be in our place soon.

Blue Light: My work is over. I am passing the baton.

I was sad. By this time, the light has become my best friend. I can't imagine that he is leaving me.

Blue Light: I am not leaving you. I am inside you. Whenever you want just call me.

The light dissolved in my heart. The bull helped me to get on to it. We moved on. I could hear loud sounds of conch shells in air. The sky became brighter and the atmosphere warmer.

The bull told me stories about the mountain and ashram. The bull has been living here since ages. He is a Swayambhu bull. Maha Guru wanted a strong guard to the place. Once asuras started assaulting students. Guru requested Shiva to send a bull to protect the place. From that day, this bull never moved from the gate of the school. There is only one season in the premises- autumn i.e., not so warm or not so cold. It was difficult to believe that. In the middle of Himalayas, with harsh cold, how can only one place have an autumn season.

I saw ashram from distance. It looked like a diamond. A golden light was emanating from it to all directions. I saw two globes above that place. It was sun and moon. God, what all magics are waiting for me. I saw hundreds of people coming out of the school and going to different directions.

The big door opened with a loud sound. Ashram was calm. I could not see anyone. I got down.

A background voice-

"You can take bath, eat food, chant Gayathri Mantra for 1 Lakh times and sleep for the day. Your training will start from tomorrow. Maha Guru instructs you to get up at Brahma Muhurta and meet him"

That was the beginning of a 6-year long training. I forgot my past. I dropped all my baggage and immersed in the ganga of knowledge.

Chapter - 20

The sun rises at 3 O clock there. Everyone should wake up by that time. You can see people walking around for morning ablutions. There is a water fall in the ashram and bath can be done there. Sandhya Vandana followed by Surya Namaskar and some secret mantras comes next. When I was ready for the training, the bull came to pick me.

Me: Where were you, Kesava? I felt so lonely yesterday.

Kesava: You have to lead your life alone. I may not be with you always.

Kesava replied with a smile. That is true. My stay here is temporary.

Kesava took me to a far place. It was deep inside a forest. He dropped me in a valley.

Kesava: You may sit on the rock there and do meditation. Maha Guru will call you once you are matured to imbibe his words. I am leaving.

Without even looking at me, he left. I was scared. That was a faraway place from the ashram and I was alone there. Even in that morning, darkness was omnipresent.

I sat in padmasana, with closed eyes. By that time, I abhorred eating and drinking. My conviction on nature grew leaps and bounds. My body adapted to the

Himalayan weather, aided by the training of Kashi Swamiji.

Time zone stood silent for me. I saw the universe in my tapas. With each mantra, I was dragged closer to the nature.

One day, I heard a soft voice- "Son, you may discontinue your Japa. Time has come for the training". It was Maha guru and upon seeing him, I melt inside. I have never seen a person with so much grace and energy.

Guru: Son, look at yourself and see the changes.

He showed a cup of water.

I became younger. Beard became thicker and face was glowing. My hands touched his feet.

Guru: Bharath Matha has been waiting for you since long. We were eager to see you, my son.

Me: I can hear my inner soul.

Guru: Good, we will start our training tomorrow. You may take rest today. Kesava will come and drop you at our ashram.

Guru informed me that I have been doing tapas for almost 1 year and should feel good about it. His words were soothing and gave me the courage to fight challenges.

The next day, I had the opportunity to talk to the people of ashram. All of them were new joiners. By seeing them itself, I could know about their details like birth place, family and age.

Out of the crowd, I liked two people- One Aditya and Amith. We became close friends. There were many common things except age. They were younger to me.

Guru: You are going to learn Bharath Veda- The fifth one. It is very sacred and only few people in this world know about this. General public knows about only 4 Vedas which Kashi Swami taught you. But Vyasa wrote this and kept as a secret.

Me: What was the reason for it?

Guru: This one is very much powerful and can be misused. Bharath is the center of energy of this universe. A person with knowledge of this can protect her from any bad influence. This is written only for the purpose of security of Bharath.

Me: If Bharath is the center of power, she can protect herself, right?

Guru: Good question. In this world there are Asuras who want to capture her and rule. They constantly get energized from other part of the universe. This world is very big and it has a darker part. We are living on the brighter and revered part. Asuras are living on the central part. They go to the darker part and do black magic.

Guru Said....

Kashi Swami taught you 4 Vedas in five days. But you can't learn Bharath Veda like that. It will take time. Be ready for it. This is the most difficult Veda. One of the students of Vyasa Acharya is sitting on the top of the earth and always reciting it. At times he forgets the verses. Taking advantage of it, Asuras attack our country.

Our country was ruled by English, Portuguese, Dutch, French, Afghans, Turks, Mangols and many more. All these are manifestations of Asuras. When British ruled us, their country prospered. When Turks ruled us, they ruined our wealth. Everyone wants our natural resources. Once we were the richest. We were far ahead in terms of culture and thinking. We were home to all refugees. Now what is the situation? We are called third world country.

Even today, we are facing tests. So only people like you can uplift our nation. This is necessary for the overall good of this universe. Hindustan is the sanctum sanctorum of nature.

Hope you appreciate the importance of your stay here. I see you as Sree Krishna who can drive this country to greater heights.

After completion of your studies, you can go back to your village. You will be a normal man then and will remember Bharath Veda only in need. Life will be in trouble for a long time but at the end, you will be placed in the highest position.

You will also get into the company of people who will support you in this mission. They are also being trained here for the task.

Me: Guru, I will use this Veda for the prosperity of our country. I will ensure that I leave no stone unturned to achieve our goals.

Guru Said,

You will get guidance and instructions from time to time from here. I have been living here for 5000 years. I have seen my mother crying and can't take it anymore.

I would like to tell you some truths.

After Bharath got independence from English, they left this country with hesitation. They plundered us for centuries and were greedy for more. They created a plan to subject us to perpetual control. They left their imprints here. They also mandated a set of people throughout Bharath to spread their culture. The idea was to manufacture slave mentality. There are politicians who make illegal money here and send to them.

Acharya Sabha of Himalayas sensed the danger and we prayed to Trimurthies. We did heavy penance for years. They had no other option but to appear before us.

Do you know what they offered us?

They promised us to take incarnation again and come to this country. The avatar will be simple and they will live among people. Nobody will notice them for years. People with super natural powers will also be not able to identify them. They will have to make lot of sacrifices. There is no clarity if they have already taken birth or not. This is above our vision. They will join you at appropriate time.

Maha Guru stopped and closed his eyes.

A thunder went past by my body. What am I hearing?

My advent with the Veda was done on an auspicious time. The verses were difficult. These are words which are not normally used in transactional Sanskrit. Learning words took time. Me, Aditya and Amit were quick to grasp.

The Fifth Veda

Aditya was the better among us. He was a Sanskrit student at Kashi.

My inner vision talks about Aditya and Amit.

Aditya was born to a business family at nondescript village in Madhya Pradesh. From childhood, his interest was to become a Sanskrit teacher. He never went to school. His master was a guru in a nearby ashram. He taught Aditya all verses in Sanskrit. Aditya wished to continue in that ashram and spend a common life. One day his guru called and shouted at his for no reason. He asked Aditya to get out form the Ashram and never come again. With filled eyes, he left the place. This was the trick of the guru to send him to Himalayas. Aditya wandered here and there and joined this ashram at the end.

Amit started as a street goonda at Haryana. He being an orphan, had no means to live. Having good physique, he joined a local gang. The team had an altercation with a swami in the area. Amit was sent to assault the hermit. Amit fell unconscious at his place and was lying on swami's lap when he was back to senses. The guru asked Amit to escape from the gang and go to Kedarnath. Amit met another person at Kedar who directed him to this place.

Time passed like seasons. The ashram was the most peaceful and beautiful at any time. We did not know where it starts and where it ends. We saw many animals and birds living in concord. There was no scarcity of food. Nobody worked for money but abundance was palpable. Emotions never disturbed us. We had only one idea- The rise of Hindustan.

I was eating a fruit at Ashram. Message from guru says- Please come and meet me at the rock.

Rock is the place where guru intimates an important note to the pupil. I waited for an hour for the guru .

Guru: Kalachakra is so fast. It does not wait for anyone. It does its karma and keeps on ticking. You were directed here few years back and your studies are complete.

I was shocked to hear it. Kesava once stated- Bharath Veda in not taught in full. Guru assesses one's capability and teaches parts of the text. Only Mahadeva, Vishnu, Brahma and Maha Guru know it completely. Students of Bharath Veda are given intimation when their training is done.

Guru: You are the first student to completely go through this session.

I thanked the nature who gave me this opportunity to understand this text. What next?

Guru: You can go back to your Karma Kshetra and do seva of Matha.

Me: Guru, do not abandon me. I want to live under your feet.

I cried.

Guru: You are not a jnana yogi but a karma yogi. You have a lot of work in Bharath. There is an impending danger on Her. It is your duty to overcome that.

Guru touched my head. I was inconsolable. My soul was interwoven in the ashram. There is a NIYOGA for all and it is time. My mind said. Why are you weeping?

Guru: You will be back to normal after stepping out from here. Kesava will take you till the foot hills. Take a dip at Hima Kund again and you will find your way home. After you arrive at your village, you can lead a normal life. You will not be able to recollect the Veda. You will get guidance from us about your work. Whenever you or Mata gets into trouble, the Veda will reappear in your heart. Do Sandhya Vandan daily. You will encounter problems in your home village. You will be in our radar. So, time to move has come.

Maha Guru disappeared. I felt lonely. Nobody was there in the ashram. I could not see Amith and Aditya. I will have to go without saying bye to the inhabitants. An eerie silence gripped the area. Kesava was standing at the entrance. Even he did not seem to be emotional. I sat on him.

A background voice said- You are the only student with permission to come back to this place. We will call you back when time comes.

Kesava's legs took strides. We were descending.

Chapter - 21

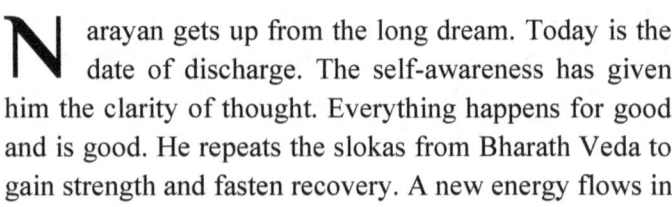

Narayan gets up from the long dream. Today is the date of discharge. The self-awareness has given him the clarity of thought. Everything happens for good and is good. He repeats the slokas from Bharath Veda to gain strength and fasten recovery. A new energy flows in his body. A fresh light glows in his eyes and the missionary zeal reverberates in his heart.

Narayan is taking rest in his house. The wounds are gone. Tamil visits him daily. Nanda and Parvathi are happier than ever. Seetha passed her exams with good marks. The family is safe and secure. The owl on the tree has gone away. Angai cooks healthy meals for Narayan.

Death of Brahma was a rude shock to Narayan. Brahma, the poor fellow, was a pawn. The King and the Prime Minister are in jail. There is a rumor that they may take release on parole in a month.

Midnight…Narayan sleeps on the bed. There is an inner calling. He wakes up. The blue light shines like a star. Besides it, Maha Guru sits.

Maha Guru: The Niyoga has knocked your doors. The Veda will be always in your memory from now. The country is in trouble.

Guru Says,

Britishers left us physically but they are still operating here. We were the most profitable investment for them. So, even after 25 years they plan to ruin us. They have their agents here. Along with Britishers, other powers are also in tandem to see our down fall. They have intruded into our administrative machinery from top to bottom. Businessmen from west are sponsoring it and they are getting excellent returns. Poor in our country are remaining poor. It is your duty to cleanse the rot.

Guru Continues….

Two Britishers have come to regain control of our country. They are sent with clear mandate to create chaos. Your current job is to restrict them and make them flee.

Let me explain you how the work has been till now.

A European has entered the most powerful political family of our country. He has married the daughter of the strong man. The strong man and his associates were part of the English plan from the outset. Since they failed to capture the psyche of our country as Bharath Veda students acted as bulwark to their efforts, they formed a long-term strategy. The European got in touch with the girl when she was a graduate student of a college in London. Slowly he developed relationship with her. The story culminated in their marriage. He converted to Hinduism and has come to India as a groom. He has started to exert control over the Nationalist Party. His orders are being executed there and obviously they are anti Indian. He lives in London and has a remote control over us.

A gang of patriots and freedom fighters within the Nationalist Party has smelled the rat. They are being thrown out of their posts and sidelined. Lot of black money is generated and is deposited to an English Bank. If this continues, we will be in ruins. They even have an idea to exterminate the opposition. Helicopter crashes and road accidents may hog our headlines.

The European and his associates has decided to generate speedy output. Next two years India will boil. They have convinced the PM to crush dissent and curtail rights. Another plan is to castrate maximum people so that population won't grow.

After waves of this episode will affect next 10 years. By that time, India will fall back to pre-British era. Antidote to this is your action for next 60 years.

You have to wither stones thrown at us. How long can this country be enslaved? A millennium has gone under darkness. Lights of countless families went off. Tears from our women equaled waters in Ganga. The Bharath Mata lost her jewel in the crown, her arms. Ornament in her feet. Enough, Narayan, you are brought to this world to save Her from further fall…to bring her treasure back…to raise the golden bird again.

Narayan: What should I do, Guru?

Guru: You will have to start another journey but this time for Kurukshetra. You will get company of Blue Light till you are joining the army which will wage this war. You should intimate your family about the travel. Be in touch with them and they will be happy. All the best, son.

Maha Guru dissolved in air.

Narayan gets up and packs his bag. He takes a bath and does prayer. He goes to temple and stands in silence. Kali Ma will be happy on his assignment. He takes a turn and sees Muthu, Nachiar, Chettiar and Muthu's guru.

He falls at their feet.

Chettiar: We exhausted all our knowledge to discover you but we failed.

Nachiar: But we are sure that you are a sacred birth and you will touch the sky.

Guru: We know that you are going in exile. We are sure that you will do only good to this country.

Muthu: Come back soon and with success.

Muthu holds him tight and smiles.

Muthu: We will come with you till your home.

Nanda and Parvathy are speechless. Happiness was about to grow in their home. Tamil and Seetha are speaking with wet eyes.

Chettiar: He is going to continue his studies at Varanasi, right. You all should be happy.

Parvathy takes a bag of food and keeps it in the travel pack. Chettiar takes Narayan to a corner. He gives him few currency notes.

Chettiar: Inform me if you need more.

Narayan to Tamil: We are one and will remain one. Give me time till I finish my work. I will come and take you with me.

He does not know where to go. As per the communique from Maha Guru, Blue Light will show the way. Narayan waits for the light to originate. Nanda and Parvathy are thinking if Narayan is in a dilemma.

Soon the Blue Light emerges from his heart and waves at him. It starts to move…Narayan without looking back, follows the light…The journey is to a long future…. The time to decide the fate of millions of Indians….

The radio plays a news then….

PM has declared emergency…Fundamental rights are suspended…Associations are banned……

Narayan walks ahead…. ahead and ahead.

Epilogue

"Thank you, Bhai, how much should I pay?"

Cab Driver: Rs 500.

AP: Your story is worth more than this.

I paid him Rs 1000.

Cab Driver: Thank you, Sir, May god bless you.

AP: Forgot to ask your name.

Cab Driver: I am Suresha.

A week later, New Delhi,2024.

Ram was away for this whole week. He called me to his cabin. I doubted myself when he told me this- "You are hereby given the task of interviewing the PM".

Surprise…...!!!! I ran back to my cabin and started my preparation.

I was very much upbeat with the intimation of Ram. Though I am an experienced journalist, getting an opportunity to interview the PM was joyful for me. I read books about him. Also, I collected maximum articles written on him. I considered this as an acclaim of the sweat I dropped for the betterment of our newspaper. My wife, another reporter in the same media, was also appreciative of my feat. She cautioned me not to be over excited.

Me: Thank you, PM, for giving us the time to meet and talk to you. Let us discuss about your achievements.

PM: There is nothing called personal achievements in social work. Whatever we do is for the society.

Me: What was your ambition during childhood? Did you ever dreamt of politics and being at the helm.

PM: My wish was to support my family financially. I never wanted to come out of my village. Every life on this earth takes birth with a mandate. You like it or not, it will drag you and there are no options.

Me: What is your idea about the development of this country? You have done a lot to the people and what will be your work for next 5 years?

PM: Look. We were the richest country in ancient times. Our GDP was almost 30% of world output. We were nurturing great minds at Nalanda and Taksha Shila. Arts, culture, science and many branches of knowledge thrived here. Industries like ship building, textiles and agriculture prospered in this great land. Powers in this world envied us and they plundered our mother. We were not hostile to outsiders. They took it to their advantage. Internal disturbances among kings played the spoil sport. Foreigners succeeded in dividing us on caste and language. Even this day, we are facing the after effects of their game. There are Indians with slave mindset. I want my country to break away from this and shine again in this world.

The infrastructure in parts of our country is underdeveloped. There are no roads, railways, bridges…I want farmers to have a stable income…I want blue flame in all kitchens, paca houses…I want clean water to be supplied to all households. Employment for all. May god give us all these.

Me: May I have some personal questions?

PM: Yes.

Me: People are curious to know about you. How do you maintain same level of energy till evening every day?

PM: I get up at 3 AM in the morning. Does Sandhya Vandana and Surya Namaskar. Above all, my focus is only on one thing- the wellbeing of my citizens, the progress of my nation… I can work 24/7 for it.

Me: I read your biography. There is no mention about your life for about 6 years from your 17th birthday. Why is it? You were not in the village? Where were you?

PM: I went for an all-India tour. I visited all states of the country and understood the geography.

Me: Why is it not recorded in any books?

PM: I left the home after a fight with my father. I never disclosed anyone regarding all these. During these times, I saw many lives. All these experiences are coming handy for me as a PM.

Me: What is your advice to your countrymen?

PM: My vision is to make Bharath great. It requires contribution from all of you. You may think that it is the duty of the government to do all these. We alone can't do anything. Your involvement, irrespective off the size will be a great push to this work. Keep your heart and mind on this activity…Do not rest till we score our goal.

We will face hurdles. Every good objective will have to pass through hard times. Do not get disheartened. Solutions to problems are encrypted in Vedas and other texts. Read them regularly so that you don't fall and if you fall, you will have remedies.

Me: PM. There are lot of mysteries around you. People believe that you are a Himalayan baba who took birth here. Some say that you are son of ganga. You take Navratri Vrath. Some others spread the idea that you are messenger of Ma Kali. What do you feel after hearing all these?

Me: I am a common man and not a god. I just work hard with a clean mind. I follow our tradition. This gives me energy. By doing all these you can rise above the ordinary. Bharath gives you everything. Only lucky souls take birth here.

I have another advice to you all. There is a blue light in everyone. It can be brought out by upasanas. Do strict penance and develop the light in you. After this, listen to your light. You will succeed.

Me: PM. Do you think we have crossed the period of challenges and are comfortable to relax?

PM: We are not…There are threats from our neighbors. Vested interest groups from within the country are pulling us to different sides. Foreigners are waiting to attack. Their guns are pointed towards us. Some are doing proxy wars by funding internal groups. Terrorism is an issue….

We have to create a strong nation and the dream is still a work in progress.

Me: How can we fight this?

PM: The real army are people; national interest should be their priority.

Secretary of Agriculture Department comes in. There is some urgent work to be completed. He is waiting for the PM.

PM: What happened Sumit? Anything urgent?

Sumit: Yes, Sir. The file is to be signed today. After your sign, a lot of work needs to be done before issuing orders.

PM: Come and show me.

PM to me: Just two minutes…

Lot to be learnt from this man. My admiration for him exceeded… Every citizen of this country should get a chance to meet him. You can go back with a doubly charged mind that will work for this nation. He has only one end to meet… to make this nation the most admired one…to provide a life of dignity to our people… to shun the slavery mindset… to make the flag fly high… to make Bharath the knowledge house… because if Bharath is peaceful, the world is peaceful…. He is doing pooja of this universe… Vasudeiva Kudumbakam… Loka Samastha Sukino Bhavanthu…

PM collects the file, checks it and signs at the bottom.

Below the signature, writes his name…. Narayan Nandakumar.

www.ingramcontent.com/pod-product-compliance
Lightning Source LLC
LaVergne TN
LVHW041847070526
838199LV00045BA/1474